CHANGE **UP**

How Top Executives
Lead Change and
Deliver Results

CHANGE ^{UP}

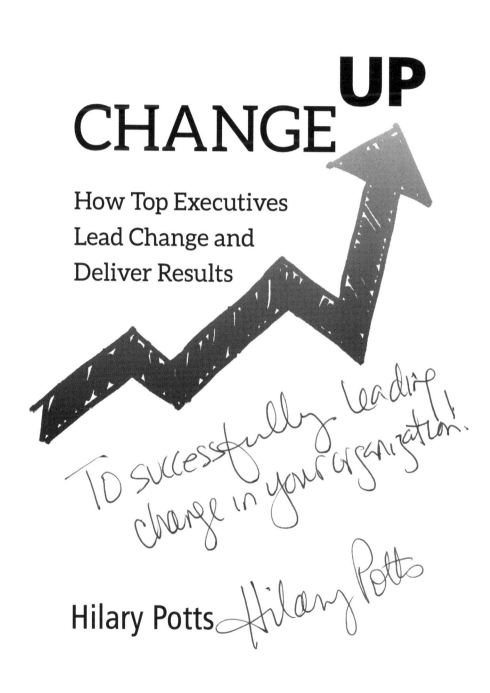

How Top Executives Lead Change and Deliver Results

To successfully lead change in your organization!

Hilary Potts *Hilary Potts*

DISCLAIMER

This book should be used only as a general guide and not as the ultimate source of the information contained herein. You as the leader will know best what will work in your particular business situation.

Copyright © 2019 by Hilary Potts

Printed in the United States of America

ISBN: 9781726772006
Imprint: Independently published

LCCN: 2018912378

Cover and Interior Design and Illustrations by Lynn Amos
Copyedited by Mark Woodworth

Requests for permission to make copies of any part of this work may be made to:
The HAP Group, Middlebury, CT
info@hapgrp.com

To Mom, who no matter what is going on

always finds the time to listen. Through her power of listening,

problems dissolve and solutions emerge.

Contents

Figures

Memos

Introduction

Most Leaders Struggle with Leading Change— and It Costs Businesses Billions

Seventy percent of strategic change initiatives fail; the research tells us that this percentage has been constant for decades. The intent behind these strategic change initiatives has been to deliver better results. When one initiative doesn't work, another one is put in its place, with hopes and prayers that this new one will yield better results.

What if you could consistently be among the 30% of leaders who successfully execute strategic initiatives? What would this mean for your company, your customers, your shareholders, and even your career?

In today's fast-paced business environment, continuous and serial change inevitably occurs. People struggle to keep up. Repeatedly, I see leaders missing the opportunity to step in and lead the change to achieve better results that they desire. Change starts when a leader is willing to come forward and take action. Unfortunately, I find leaders talk about the changes others need to make…and leave themselves out of the picture. Too often, they expect the announcement of a new strategy or plan to be enough to get people onboard and working in the new way. However, making the change stick requires finding ways to engage the hearts and minds of the people, and this means leading *differently*.

Imagine that you could work with your management team to gain agreement and alignment across the organization to quickly get traction on your strategic initiatives. What if you could build acceptance, so people "want" to be part of their successful implementation? This book gives leaders the Toolkit to successfully lead change.

Change Leadership vs. Change Management

There is a difference between "change leadership," which provides a way for leaders to think, strategize, plan, and have accountability for executing the changes, and "change management," which is a set of processes, tools, and techniques for controlling and keeping a change effort on track. Change management is only part of the solution; it is not enough by itself to implement a project.

Leaders play an extremely important role in ensuring that the strategic initiative delivers the results. This requires stepping in at the right times, in the right ways, to lead and guide the transition from the old way to the new way of doing things. Leading change involves thinking about how all the business initiatives work together and how your fellow leaders and employees will be actively engaged to achieve the overall results.

Leaders frequently take themselves out of the implementation by delegating, even abdicating, responsibility for the deployment of an important business initiative to the change management team. Some leaders may announce and launch the change, look for a "quick win," and move on to the next business challenge before the results have been fully realized. Meanwhile, people throughout the organization struggle to figure out what to do, and as a result the change initiative cannot be sustained.

The Truths I've Learned About Leading Change

I have learned some consistent truths about leading change, regardless of the type of company, the industry, the size of the business, or the location. Over the last few decades, I have worked with senior leaders on hundreds of strategic enterprise initiatives, from mergers-and-acquisitions to reorganizations to executing new strategies. I've seen what works, what leads to problems—and what can be fixed.

It's no surprise that people are the critical asset in successfully leading change. Leaders who know how to navigate and lead change with and through others have a competitive advantage that enables them to reap the rewards of increased revenue and profits. Unfortunately, most leaders, while they may be constantly initiating change, admit they are neither very good at it nor comfortable with leading it. They, and you, may benefit from knowing the hard truths about leading change, including:

- **Change starts with leadership.** Leaders talk about what others need to do to implement the change, but don't always realize that change starts with themselves. Additionally, leaders are not always comfortable with change. Change initiatives succeed when leaders accept the change, are actively involved in it, and are accountable for the results.

- **Change is disruptive and messy.** People can get distracted and resist the change. Leaders can help their people stay away from gossiping, so they can focus instead on what matters to drive positive outcomes.

- **A company's people and culture influence the outcomes.** The business content can consume leaders' time, so the people aspects get shortchanged. Strategic changes succeed or fail based on the culture and the people. Simply put, what people do and say will impact the business results. Therefore, leading change requires using both business and people skills to gain the benefits of the change.

- **People want the benefits of change, but do not want to actually *be* changed.** Change requires getting people ready, willing, and able to "want" to make the change. This may mean that they must learn new behaviors. Therefore, if you want a different outcome, you must change what you and your people do. Leaders can accelerate the change process by helping people see "what's in it for them" through the right positive reinforcement.

- **Change efforts fail in the handoffs.** Many change efforts fail when the handoff from the project team to the leadership team isn't clear, or when leaders fail to accept full accountability for executing the plans.

Common Mistakes Leaders Make When Leading Change

Change, by definition, means "to make or become different." Change means to alter, adjust, modify, or refine. When you implement change, you are asking your people to act and behave differently; you are asking them to adapt to a new way of working. Your actions are essential for creating the conditions for change. Too frequently, though, I find that leaders don't know how to create those conditions, they make mistakes, or they have misperceptions or misinformation. Regrettably, too many leaders shy away from the human side of change.

One of the goals of this book is to help you identify where you and your leadership team may need to pay more attention to how you engage in the change. Figure 1 shows the 10 most common mistakes I've seen leaders make when leading change. Review these 10 mistakes to determine where you and your team may get off track.

Leaders' Common Mistakes

1. **Miscalculating their role in executing strategic changes:** Leaders work on plans they expect others to carry out. Leaders want the results of a strategic initiative, but may not see the need to change their *own* actions to be part of the change effort.

2. **Thinking strategy is enough:** Many leaders consider strategy and project plans sufficient to engage organizations in implementing the initiative. The organization needs more, though. By itself, it cannot bridge the strategy and the plans to achieve the business outcomes.

3. **Misallocating time between creating and implementing the solution:** It is easy for leaders to spend too much time on developing the solution and then to run out of time to adequately develop and execute the plans.

4. **Implementing too many "top" priorities:** People become overwhelmed by too many initiatives that are all considered "top" priorities. Leaders need to clearly articulate how the new initiative fits in with the current projects and daily work.

5. **Believing leaders will be prepared to lead the change:** Senior leaders usually prepare for announcing the change. However, they often spend less time preparing and cascading messages, which would enable their full leadership team to consistently communicate the information. As a result, the announcement leads to more questions to which leaders are not adequately prepared to respond.

Figure 1

Leaders' Common Mistakes

6. **Disengaging from the implementation:** When leaders are not fully engaged in the implementation, people may not take the initiative seriously. Leaders must be available or at least visible to observe what is going on and to answer questions that will support the implementation.

7. **Assuming that "telling" people what to do will produce action:** Just because people are informed about the change doesn't mean they will take action. Change usually requires people to act and behave differently. People may need additional, ongoing information, as well as guidance and feedback, before they can carry out their parts successfully.

8. **Lacking agreement and alignment across the leadership team:** Leaders don't always agree about *what* to accomplish, *why* it's important to handle this now, and *how* the organization will implement the solution. This causes confusion throughout the organization. As a result, functions, departments, and even entire regions are left to interpret how to implement the initiative.

9. **Ignoring the natural resistance to change:** When people hear about a change, it's natural for them to ask questions to clarify what's happening. Every person processes and adapts to change at a different rate. If leaders ignore or avoid people who sound as if they are disagreeing, these leaders may miss an opportunity to help them overcome any objections and move to engage in a viable solution. Leaders can reduce the churn created by a change and can accelerate progress by addressing questions and concerns upfront.

10. **Discounting smaller initiatives as inconsequential:** Leaders are inclined to think that smaller initiatives can be successfully implemented without incorporating change strategies. But all business changes, regardless of size, require behavioral changes if they are to be successful. A smaller project or a series of small projects on their own may look insignificant, but they can have a profound impact on employee actions.

Figure 1, continued

The best way to avoid these common mistakes is to create a leadership change strategy and set of plans so that you know what to do, when to get involved, and how to engage in executing your strategy. This book provides practical steps and tools to incorporate the Five Keys for Leading Change into your preparation and execution of business changes.

Leading Change

Change takes people out of their comfort zone. Some people like it, but most would prefer doing things the way they always have done, even when it's clear that change is needed. In my writing and consulting work, I lay out the Five Keys for Leading Change and give leaders a lens to lead the people side of change. These Keys serve as a way to observe and assess whether you and your people are moving through the change process and where people could use your support. The Five Keys for Leading Change shown in Figure 2 give leaders a simple diagnostic tool to assess individual and group readiness for implementing the change. Let's look closely at these Keys.

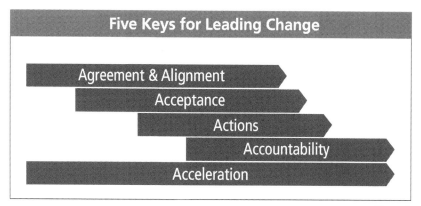

Figure 2

Accountability. When you accept accountability for a change, you chart a course and model new behaviors. You communicate, coach, and provide feedback to get people to work in the new way; and you build accountability throughout the organization, so that multiple leaders and employees are responsible for results.

Agreement & Alignment. Because of different perspectives, leadership teams may struggle to gain consensus about what to do and how to implement a change effort. With agreement, the leadership team has a shared view of the future. Agreement is about "what" you want to do and "why" it is important.

Agreement isn't sufficient by itself, though. You and your team need to align around how the organization will navigate and adopt the new way of working so that everyone's actions are moving in the desired direction. When business functions, such as sales, operations, and marketing, are left to figure it out for themselves, implementation can be sporadic and disjointed, potentially adding costs to the initiative and sometimes even leading to failure to meet the desired results.

Acceptance. Your role is to get people engaged and committed to the change. Help people understand what will happen, why it's important, and what they can do to be part of the solution. When people are positively motivated to accept and make a change, they move more quickly into the new way of working.

Unfortunately, during times of change, some people can become paralyzed or resistant to the very changes that can help both them and the business thrive. People process changes differently—mentally, emotionally, and physically. You can help by sharing what's going to happen and by providing safe places for people to talk about their concerns as well as discuss how they can engage in new actions without feeling vulnerable.

Actions. New behaviors often feel awkward. Competing priorities can get in the way. You can help people take the right actions by focusing them on the right priorities and reinforcing new behaviors. This requires you to understand what people need to start doing differently and what they no longer need to do. This may require new approaches to getting the work done.

Acceleration. Your people are the key assets for accelerating results. When you actively engage with them, they can accelerate results through consistent actions and seeing actions through to results. It's about removing obstacles and providing support and feedback as people work in a new way.

The Five Keys help you assess whether you are building engagement, accountability, and productivity for the change effort. The Keys will serve as a quick reference, even a leadership lens, for ensuring that your people will be ready, willing, and able to execute the change. The Keys are meant to be used throughout the execution of the initiative, to help you understand what's working—and what's off track.

Why a Toolkit?

The Toolkit in this book gives you the practical tips, tools, and techniques for translating the strategy and business plans into specific leadership actions. The various components in the Toolkit also help you know personally when and how you should engage in the implementation of a change effort. I tell my clients: if your people are involved in the change, you probably need strategies and plans to lay out the specific leadership actions you need to take to get your people to support the effort.

The development of the components in the Toolkit facilitates the conversations among the leadership team on strategizing, preparing, and leading both the business side and the people side of strategic change initiatives. The Toolkit prompts you to consider the impact that the change initiative has on other ongoing work and on the organization itself. The intent is to identify the issues and obstacles ahead of time and to build the right leader actions into the implementation of the change effort. It isn't enough to just lay out various project and change plans. The plans need to be translated into specific leadership actions to be carried out. The components in the Toolkit help you know how to take a more active role to keep all the aspects of the initiative on track.

The Five Keys are incorporated into the components of the Toolkit. The Toolkit is devised in such a way that you and others in your leadership team can gain agreement and alignment, and can help people understand and accept the change, so that they will take action and assert ownership of the new way. By working through the components of the Toolkit with them, you can support the passing of the baton from the project and change teams to your leadership team, which is ultimately accountable for implementing the solution. As you incorporate the Five Keys into your approach to leading change, you will develop a clear roadmap for leading change that is right for your organization.

The Toolkit consists of key change components, as shown in Figure 3, which take leaders from the concept to execution to achievement of the end results. This book outlines the steps for developing the change components, to minimize the complications that can arise when leading others during times of change. Through using the Toolkit, you identify specific actions you can take to keep the initiative moving and to accelerate business outcomes.

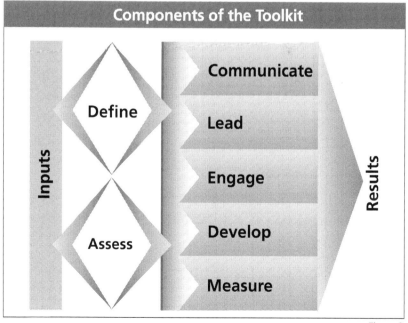

Figure 3

Leading change requires both agility and flexibility. The components of the Toolkit are designed to be an iterative process. As you work on one aspect of the Toolkit, you will find yourself adjusting other components. Businesses are wholes, not parts, so all divisions, departments, and functions within the business, along with any external factors, should eventually be covered. That way, you can develop a fully effective Toolkit for leading change.

Throughout this book, I provide discussion questions and worksheets, to provide visual cues for how to build your leadership change plans. This approach works for the majority of cases. However, these templates can—and likely should—be altered to meet your company and the specific initiative. Because each business is different, it is important to build tools that work for *you* and that provide the guidance you and your leadership team need in specific initiatives.

A Case Study Approach to Creating a Leader Change Toolkit

I use a fictional but typical case study to illustrate what to consider when developing your leadership plans. This approach draws on the strategy and project implementation plans to identify leadership actions, as well as sticking points, misalignment, or conflicts. The components of the Toolkit are not a substitute for the project and implementation plans, but rather sit above them and focus on the actions of the leader.

A merger-and-acquisition (the creation of a company we'll call MergeCo) was chosen for the case study, as most mergers-and-acquisitions, whether large or small, involve many business complexities, comprise a variety of leadership considerations, and require people to make changes. As you work through this case study, I hope you will find yourself thinking about and discussing your approach to leading change across a wide breadth of scenarios that may apply to your own business. While the case study outlines a manufacturing business, you will recognize that many of the challenges the leaders are facing have little to do with industry-specific issues; rather, they are the typical challenges all leaders face, regardless of industry or geography. Each chapter of this book includes memos that update what was happening at MergeCo over the course of the first year after the merger, which suggest some of the challenges and issues its leaders had to deal with.

Additional case studies are included in the appendices to illustrate other change challenges and the approaches a variety of leaders took in using the Toolkit components to actively engage with their people to get and keep their initiative on track.

How to Get the Most Out of This Book

Overall this book will help you:

- Create a leadership change strategy that helps you know when, where, and how to engage in the change effort

- Map out strategies to gain agreement, alignment, and acceptance for the change, which accelerate actions and build accountability for the strategic initiative

- Work with your leadership team to facilitate discussions to successfully move from planning to execution to results by leading both the business and the people aspects of a change initiative

There are several ways you can use this book. My advice is to start at the beginning and work your way through. Read both the "What You Need to Know" and "Focus on the Case Study" sections in each chapter; then work through the case study discussion questions at each chapter's end.

If you proceed through the book from beginning to end, you will develop a deep understanding of how the components of the Toolkit work, so that you can map out your leadership change strategy and plans. While this book is sequenced in an order that works for most businesses, I always encourage leaders to work in the order that they and their team have the motivation and interest to tackle. Therefore, you may prefer to read through the content in "What You Need to Know" in each chapter and then apply it directly to your situation. Otherwise, you can skip around to areas that you see as your biggest pain points. The key to success is to address *all* the aspects of the Toolkit so that you can create a complete picture of the change you wish to have happen.

Each case study is designed to help you think through how the Toolkit can help you execute your strategic initiatives. After you work through the case study in chapters 1 through 12, you'll find in Appendix A an outline for incorporating the Five Keys into your leadership discussions. Read Appendix B: What Really Happened at MergeCo for further insights into the book's case study. Appendices C and D provide additional case study examples: a successful merger-and-acquisition, and a strategic reorganization in which leaders used the Toolkit components to create a roadmap to achieve their business outcomes.

My hope is that you and your leadership team find this strategic approach to leading change beneficial and that your change efforts yield results which exceed your expectations. Additional resources designed to help you and your team to execute strategic change initiatives can be found at **www.hapgrp.com**.

For My Change Management and Project Management Experts: "Change management" includes vast bodies of knowledge, tools, and techniques. This book focuses on "change leadership": those critical leadership actions that drive successful change. It does not attempt to cover the change management process itself. Nor is it meant to replace the fine work you yourself already do. There is an emphasis on the handoffs from the project and change teams to the leaders, which are often missed when using traditional change management plans.

This book is intended to act as a guide for leaders, giving them the leadership strategies and tools to assess and understand their role in leading change—something that is often ignored or missed entirely in change initiatives. My hope is that leaders who apply the Five Keys for Leading Change and the tools this book presents will be much more proactively engaged in leading the way to better results.

THE CASE STUDY

MergeCo's Story

An industrial manufacturing company in the northern United States (which we'll call NorthCo) had long been successful in its traditional marketplace but saw both declining opportunities for growth and a changing marketplace, especially in global markets. It decided to identify and merge with another manufacturing company with similar success and complementary capabilities. A team of executives looked for potential merger partners and identified a company in the southern United States (called SouthCo).

NorthCo's CEO approached SouthCo's CEO, and the two started a series of conversations, leading to the intention to merge. Both CEOs knew that mergers are notoriously difficult to pull off, but they thought that through careful planning they could make it work. They put together a confidential team of top executives from each company to plan the merger.

The two CEOs set out for their respective Boards the benefits that would result from the merger: increased growth potential, shared Research and Development (R&D), greater marketplace presence, coordinated supply chains and manufacturing, and smoother distribution logistics, among other things. The main benefit of the merger would be leveraging the size and scope of the combined entities to achieve greater marketplace success. NorthCo saw the merger as an opportunity to expand into international markets where SouthCo's innovative product line would be attractive to external markets. An additional potential benefit would be realizing a perceived $1B in cost savings from combining processes and operations. This cost savings could self-fund future product development.

Both Boards agreed to the merger, believing that the combination of

NorthCo and SouthCo would make the new company (MergeCo) a formidable competitor in the marketplace.

NorthCo's CEO was named as the CEO of the merged company, but he pledged in announcement communications that this would be a merger of equals. The SouthCo CEO was asked to stay on for two years, and he agreed to act as NorthCo's second-in-command and lead the integration. Both Boards expressed concerns that while this was a merger, they wanted to make sure that the best practices would be used for MergeCo, and even new ones created. The two CEOs knew they should move quickly to create the merged company, MergeCo. They named an executive committee and put together approximately 50 teams of leaders from both companies to work on aspects of the merger integration of the companies. Both companies announced the merger, and the transaction closed without any issues.

However, at the end of the first month, executives and employees in both companies expressed unease about the merger. Almost from the beginning, it became clear that this was *not* a merger of equals; rather, NorthCo regarded itself as and was acting as an acquirer, rather than as a merger partner. The core business decisions were being made from NorthCo's headquarters, and its executives dominated the merger teams. The implementation of financial controls and reporting, which NorthCo thought were clear and agreed to, was causing concerns at SouthCo about compliance, authority, and decision rights.

It soon became increasingly clear that the cultures of the two companies varied significantly. NorthCo was a long-established northern industrial company. It was a highly structured organization, with strict lines of authority and decision rights, and its company rules acknowledged the presence of a strong union as having certain powers. NorthCo's customers were mostly northern companies like itself. By contrast, SouthCo was only 20 years old, founded by a team of executives that moved to the South to get away from the formal northern industrial culture and unionization. SouthCo had a reputation in the marketplace for being agile and innovative, with lots of new technology in the pipeline. SouthCo's customers tended to be smaller companies in the South and West, with more relaxed purchasing processes and requirements. These differences in products and market-place approaches would make combining the sales forces problematic.

After MergeCo's Day One of operations, little integration progress was made. There was no clear integration strategy. Business units and functions were simply charged with figuring out how to merge their respective areas. The clashing cultures and different leadership styles interfered with the work of the merger teams. Each side was used to working in certain ways, according to its own culture. When NorthCo executives on the teams started to exert authority, SouthCo's executives resisted. This dynamic meant that important integration actions were delayed—or did not happen at all.

With much of the merger conversation and work occurring at the executive level, leaders and employees throughout both organizations did not under-stand what was happening, what their roles would be going forward, and whether they would even have jobs in a few months. While both companies held merger announcement town halls and sent a follow-up memo from the two CEOs, people hadn't heard anything else. With the delays in the work of the merger teams, no further communications were being issued about specific integration work. Employees felt unsettled, particularly at SouthCo. Productivity declined. Employee turnover rose sharply, and many executives (some of them key to company success) left for competing companies.

At the end of six months, there was some progress toward integration: Sales was combined into one organization, the R&D teams were sharing information, and the marketing teams were moving ahead with plans covering the full range of products. Beyond these first steps, though, little had been achieved. NorthCo was acting as if it was fully in control. The

SouthCo executives on merger teams rarely attended meetings, as the merger work was turning into "NorthCo imposing its way of doing business" instead of "partners forming a combined way of doing business." Customers, stakeholders, and the business press alike appeared confused by the lack of coordination between the two companies. In effect, there *was* no MergeCo; in many ways, the two companies were continuing to operate as they had been, for lack of integrated processes and strategies. Most important, the merged Board was not seeing even the beginnings of the promised cost reductions, as there was little integration of processes and operations.

At the end of the first year, the Board and executives looked at the results: While the merger was providing some benefits (mostly in sharing R&D and in streamlining processes), the rest of the promised benefits were elusive. Most concerning to the Board and stakeholders (not to mention the marketplace), the financial results dropped, due to lack of cost reduction and marketplace confusion.

So MergeCo's CEO chartered a task force of leaders across both NorthCo and SouthCo. The taskforce was asked to analyze what had happened over the past year and to recommend options for saving the merger and delivering results. The task force was given three months to do its work. The task force agreed to start by assessing the integration strategy and focusing on specific areas, starting with the supply chain and working through reducing costs, boosting sales, and ramping up marketing to find synergies and gain additional revenues.

> The MergeCo case study highlights how to develop your change lens (using the Five Keys for Leading Change) and the components of the Toolkit. Each chapter contains a memo that provides additional information about what

happened during MergeCo's first year. As you work on the case study, you will be asked to make assumptions and fill in what you know. The point is to use the case study and discussion questions to understand how to use each component in the Toolkit to benefit your own organization.

The techniques in the Toolkit are simple. None of them are complicated. However, using the Toolkit does require some discipline in thinking, strategizing, planning, and executing actions. If you want to deliver extraordinary results by leading change, you have to be willing to let go of old habits to learn and adapt to new ones. *The change starts with you.*

PART I

Set the Context

Chapter 1
Create Your Toolkit

What You Need to Know

Many leaders deploy a project team to chart out and manage significant change initiatives. In mergers and other significant change efforts, there can be numerous teams (including subject matter experts and key individuals) working to gain the synergies, higher revenues, and cost savings for the initiative. Project plans and even change management plans are created to aid in the implementation of the solution. Usually, an executive steering committee oversees the progress.

It is often assumed that, if the project plan contains a task requiring leadership or organizational actions, leaders will do the task. Unfortunately, this isn't always the case. Often the project tasks are communicated on short notice and do not take into account the other business deliverables the leader is expected to complete in that same time frame. The key to getting the necessary work done is an effective handoff from the project team to the organization. If this handoff is not done correctly, the change initiative may fail. Pay special attention that the handoff from the project team to the organization is smooth, seamless, and effective.

The Benefits of a Toolkit

The components of the Toolkit help you think through and prepare to engage in executing the changes to accelerate the results. Instead of assuming the changes will happen merely because they are included in a project plan or announced to the organization, the components are designed to assist you and your leadership team by identifying areas of conflict, sticking points, and key interactions to pay attention to as you implement the change.

The Toolkit helps you:

- Translate the business strategy and plan into a compelling vision and case for change that yield results and that others will want to follow

- Understand and address the business, people, and organizational impacts that occur with a change

- Gain agreement, alignment, and commitment among you yourself, your leadership team, and the organization

- Lay out leadership strategies and actions required to drive and reinforce the new behaviors for achieving results

- Communicate compelling messages to engage specific stakeholders in positive actions

- Become aware of the organizational interdependencies and other implications to create a timeline that prioritizes and sequences the work

- Determine how to get people engaged by defining the behavior changes and identifying and resolving issues ahead of time

- Monitor and measure the progress to create a positive learning environment for accelerating the change

The Components of the Toolkit

The Toolkit components are usually created during the design of a strategic change effort. It is developed through a series of discussions, typically with senior leaders who are accountable for achieving the outcomes. These discussions create a visual picture, or map, that integrates the business plan, the case for change, and the project plan, as well as the communication and leadership plans that tell you and other leaders when and how to engage in the implementation of the change. The Toolkit helps you think through and monitor the change effort. Its components are your guide to ensure that the Five Keys for Leading Change are applied throughout the implementation. If you move to implement changes without attending to the Five Keys, your efforts can be met with resistance, loss of productivity, and unnecessary employee turnover, which affect overall business outcomes.

TIP: This approach, while most beneficial when used at the outset of a strategic initiative, can be employed to correct the course of a project that is not getting the traction, or the proper attention needed to deliver results. Using this methodology is a terrific way to assist you in assessing the situation and getting all leaders throughout the company engaged and working at implementing key actions.

The Toolkit provides both the structure and the flexibility to enable you to act in your business situation. For large initiatives with many separate changes, the Toolkit helps you both focus on individual areas and take an enterprise view to assess the interdependencies of multiple changes occurring simultaneously. For smaller initiatives, the Toolkit can be simplified into the core areas to be addressed. The components of the Toolkit (set out in Figure 3) help you to look at all the key aspects of leading a change and then to prepare activities and approaches that will accelerate the transition from the current ways of working to the new way. Let's take a closer look at the components. Figure 4 expands the components, so that you can see what is covered by each tool. Subsequent chapters provide more details regarding how to develop and use each component.

Components of the Toolkit (Expanded)

Collect the Inputs

- Concept/solution
- Strategy, goals
- Processes
- Project and change plans

Define the Case for Change

- Define the current and future state and why this is important to address now
- Outline measures of success
- Translate the business plan into language people can understand
- Gain agreement and alignment for the change

Assess the Business, People, and Organizational Impacts

- Assess each business element
- Complete business impact assessment
- Review the organization's history with change
- Understand the people impacts of the change initiative
- Summarize the changes— the degree of difficulty
- Prioritize and sequence those changes that need attention

Figure 4

Components of the Toolkit (Expanded)

Communicate the Change

- Develop a Communication Strategy and Plan
- Craft Big "C" and little "c" messages (internal/external, formal/informal, general and stakeholder-specific)
- Develop announcement communications
- Prepare leaders to cascade communications
- Deliver ongoing communications
- Create an information feedback system

Engage and Build Accountability

- Build acceptance
- Identify behavior changes for the new way
- Anticipate and assess the resistance, then create plans to mitigate the resistance
- Develop behavior-shaping plans
- Identify support (training tools, resources, information)
- Provide ongoing coaching and feedback

Lead the Change

- Gain agreement and alignment with your team
- Assess you and your team's change readiness
- Map out the leader role in leading the change
- Exhibit change leadership behaviors
- Support new actions with shaping plans

Measure Progress and Results

- Name leading indicators
- Establish measurement system
- Define the quantitative and qualitative measures
- Create a learning environment
- Celebrate successes, including small wins and "quick wins"

Develop a Roadmap and a Timeline

- Indicate key project actions
- Identify interdependencies
- Prioritize and sequence activities with other initiatives
- Map out pre- to post-implementation leader actions
- Incorporate communications

Assess the Results

- Celebrate progress
- Reinforce the new way
- Handle setbacks
- Incorporate lessons learned into future business changes

Figure 4, continued

Collect the Inputs. You will want to collect and review the current information that has been developed about your strategic change. Your Toolkit will be based on inputs that have already been created: the idea, solution, and strategy; the project and business plans; and the new processes or systems to be implemented. These inputs assist in the creation of the Toolkit components.

Define the Case for Change. Translate the business plan and solution into language that compels people throughout the organization to "want" to be part of the strategic change effort. A Case for Change lays out what is happening, why it's important to address an issue now, what the opportunities are, and how success will be measured in terms people can understand.

Assess and Understand the Business, People, and Organizational Impacts. Think through how proposed changes impact other business areas and work. Assess the business changes from a people perspective and analyze how these changes will affect different stakeholders and change how people do their work. Use these insights to create a Toolkit that works to move people from awareness to acceptance to action.

Communicate the Change. Convey powerful messages to enroll and enlist people to action. Go beyond the formal announcement communications to map out a communication strategy and plans to aid leaders in cascading consistent and timely messages throughout the implementation. Help leaders at every level of the company communicate in ways that build trust and gain the willingness of others to try new ways of working.

Engage and Build Accountability. Keep people focused, engaged, and productive during times of change and uncertainty. Through your actions, people can move from resistance to acceptance to action to ownership and accountability for the change. Identify the actions that help people step out of their comfort zone and try new behaviors that lead to new, beneficial results. Accelerate the change by cascading actions that reinforce a new way of working, ranging from the C-suite to the individual performer.

Lead the Change. Prepare to lead the strategic initiative in ways that bring out the best in yourself and others. People look to you for guidance, inspiration, and support. When you are actively engaged throughout the change effort, you can spot issues, remove roadblocks, and reinforce the new way and the new behaviors. This accelerates and moves the organization toward positive outcomes.

Measure Progress and Results. Use measurements to assess the effectiveness of the implementation. The measurements themselves can help people stay focused on what matters and allow the organization to positively shape the way they do their jobs. Measurements can help create a learning environment for people to try novel approaches, learn from mistakes, and celebrate successes. Identify leading indicators that provide early signals of how the results are trending.

Develop a Roadmap and a Timeline. Create a roadmap and a timeline that provide a visual picture of the key leadership activities throughout the development and execution of the effort. A roadmap guides you and your team to know what to do to lead the change effort. Use the timeline to prioritize, sort, and sequence key initiatives, leader activities, communications, and implementation touchpoints that require leader engagement.

Assess the Results. Your measurements provide some indicators—often the business-related ones—of progress. In addition to these business-related indicators, use the lens of the Five Keys to assess the people side of change. Remember that the long-term results of the change initiative depend on how the people accept the change, act to implement it, and work to accelerate the initiative. If your assessment does not show the results you expect, apply the lens of the Five Keys to determine where the problems are, then work to resolve them.

Change-savvy leaders know the importance of the "people aspects" of change. To help drive changes through the organization, they:

- Develop a compelling reason for change

- Communicate clear, inspiring messages customized for each stakeholder group

- Enlist and enroll the full leadership to implement the changes

- Drive and reinforce the new behaviors

- Create an environment where people want to learn and develop

- Remove obstacles to pave the way for peak performance

- Celebrate successes early and often

The rest of this book uses the case study to show you how to employ the Five Keys as a lens for leading a change effort. It demonstrates how to develop a well-furnished Toolkit so that you can radically increase your ability to deliver the business outcomes.

NOTES

Chapter 2

Define the Case for Change

What You Need to Know

The main truth about change is that change initiatives succeed or fail based on the culture and the people. All successful change initiatives take into account (1) how to work within the culture to move both culture and company toward the new goals and (2) how to persuade the people to change. Imagine if we were to ask two companies to implement the same strategic initiative. It is likely that the two would execute the initiatives quite differently.

People need a compelling reason to step out of their comfort zone and work in new ways. They will want to understand what's going to happen. A business plan isn't always enough to convey the messages across an organization. People will want to know what the change is, why the change is needed, and what are the results of the change. In short, people will want to understand the case for change. You will use this case for change as the basis for communicating with your leaders, management, employees, and other stakeholders.

You will refer to the case for change throughout the implementation. By reviewing the case for change, you are continuously prompted to check agreement and alignment among your colleagues to ensure that you stay true to your vision. Additionally, the Five Keys for Leading Change should be reflected in the case for change and be the foundation for executing leadership actions during the implementation.

The case for change uses the business plan as its starting point. The business plan focuses on the challenges, financial implications, and strategies for creating value and growth. The case for change translates the business strategies and plans into language people can understand. The case for change ideally will be a companion to the business plan, focusing on the degree of change, the organization's capabilities and culture, and the risks involved in making the change. You can use this case for change to bring the business plan to life for leaders and employees.

A good case for change can be used to gain agreement regarding where the organization is today, how it is going to move forward, and what the future looks like. It can start the work of the project teams and keep everyone focused and moving in the right direction. It lays out what the successful implementation will produce and how that success will be measured.

Use the following questions to facilitate a conversation to build a case for change. This will help you gain leadership agreement for the change effort.

- What is the current situation?

- What is the future vision?

- Why is it important to make this change now?

- How will we measure success (quantitatively and qualitatively)?

- Which roadblocks and risks may get in our way?

Figure 5 outlines a worksheet for capturing your ideas in brief, easy-to-read bullet points.

A compelling case for change balances the focus between what needs to be changed in the business and which changes people actually need to make for the change to be implemented successfully.

TIP: Silence can be mistaken for agreement. Head nods even can be misconstrued for approval. So, throughout the change initiative, test agreement and approval by asking questions and walking through scenarios to find out whether people are actually aligned with the case for change.

The Case for Change		
Current Situation Describe the Current Situation	**Future Vision** What Does the Future Look Like?	**Rationale** Why Is This Important Now?
How Will We Measure Success?	**What Are the Roadblocks & Risks?**	**How Will We Mitigate Risk?**

Figure 5

Focus on the Case Study

Subject: Executive Session for Our Merger Integration Team

To: MergeCo CEO (Former NorthCo CEO)

From: SouthCo Divisional President

Date: [One Month after the Merger]

I found our first team meeting two weeks ago stimulating and look forward to our second meeting. In the meantime, I have been visiting our plants and talking with our employees about the merger and all the actions that are being planned to integrate our two companies. It has surprised me that a sizable percentage of employees on both sides are not even aware that the merger is in progress; a similarly large number of employees know little about what's happening and why our two companies want to merge. These employees see two companies of different size and product lines, operating in different marketplaces, and don't understand what will come as a result of the merger. I was getting a lot of terrific questions and couldn't answer many of them.

I believe we are simply not giving people a compelling reason for this merger. We have not spent enough time laying out what we want to achieve and how the integration will work.

I firmly believe that our employees will work more productively if we take on the job of explaining to them why we're merging, who will be in charge, what the merger means to them, and why we're asking them to change their processes. We like to consider our employees as "members of our team," and to that end we should make a point of explaining, communicating, and responding to them. I know the employees on our side of the merger are looking for this type of engagement to continue. I'm confident that your employees are, as well.

I'll be glad to take the lead in drafting a "case for change" that we can use with employees to get their buy-in for this merger. It is imperative for both our companies to use consistent communications to create one company. Perhaps we can use our upcoming executive offsite meeting to discuss the case for change and other ways to engage the organization. Please let me know your thoughts.

Case Study Discussion

1. At the point of the announcement of the merger, what would you assume about the merger between NorthCo and SouthCo? What more do you need to know?

2. How do you think the MergeCo CEO responded to the SouthCo Division President? How will that response affect the work of the integration?

3. Use the template in Figure 5 to start laying out the MergeCo case for change for integrating the two businesses.

NOTES

Chapter 3
Assess the Business Impacts

What You Need to Know

NorthCo and SouthCo were two highly complex global organizations. They operated in different marketplaces with different sets of customers, competitors, and market realities. They produced different products and operated their businesses in much-different ways. The case study is clear that NorthCo and SouthCo had different cultures and leadership styles.

It comes as no surprise, then, that the two companies took very different approaches to running their respective businesses. Successfully merging the two organizations requires looking at each of the business elements and determining whether to merge one company into the other or to create a new merged entity.

A merger between the two companies would have to address the core business elements, coupled with an assessment of the external environment. The case study does not comment on the attempts of the leadership teams to understand fully the elements of the two organizations or the differences between the two sets of employees. Nor does the case study point to actions in relation to the external environments of the two companies in their different marketplaces.

Understanding the core business elements is critical in merging two entities. By comparing and contrasting how each company approaches the business and the market-place, you will uncover the differences and then assess how to move to an integrated business.

The Business's Internal and External Environments

In leading strategic changes, it is critical for leaders to understand how a shift in one business element affects what people are expected to do. Additionally, when you adjust one business element, others will be impacted.

Why is this important? For example, marketing wants to focus on new products and initiates a customer promotion, but the company does not change the sales bonus system. The sales force is given incentives to promote the older products and will lose bonus money if they transfer customers to the new products. As a result, salespeople are incentivized to continue to sell the older products and not the products on promotion.

Or consider the following situation: The IT department implements a new reporting system, which provides an easy way to gather data from field operations. Unfortunately, field operations people can't use the new system because they lack access to a company computer and have no mobile application for remote use. A terrific opportunity to gather and use information is lost without the alignment of systems and resources.

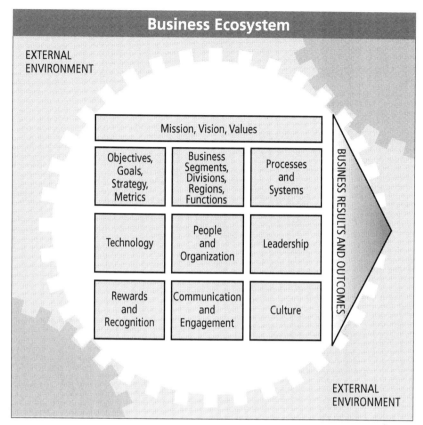

Figure 6

There are many models and ways of looking at an organization's structure, operating model, and the business elements inside it. One way is to understand that a business does not operate as a separate entity; rather, it is part of a business ecosystem. You can see this ecosystem in Figure 6, which sets out the business elements within the context of the external environment. The core business elements are presented in Figure 7. You can understand your organization better if you take a consultative, objective approach to systematically review each area. In times of change, a business might change one specific aspect of the business, such as a process change. However, it is important to understand how

Core Business Elements

Mission, Vision, Values

Objectives, Goals, Strategy, Metrics

Business Segments, Divisions, Regions, Functions

Processes and Systems

Technology

People and Organization — structure, roles and responsibilities, talent management

Leadership — philosophy, development, high-potentials, succession

Rewards and Recognition

Communication and Engagement

Culture

Business Results and Outcomes

External Environment and Contacts

Vendors and Suppliers

Figure 7

the process of change impacts other business elements, such as rewards and recognition, culture, or people.

TIP: The information just below the surface can provide deep insights into what's working (or not) and what can be improved. Be sure to investigate the interactions and interdependencies among the business elements. As you do this analysis, you will develop a stronger sense of what is involved in building your case for change. Be sure to consider which elements will be affected directly, which areas in the environment will be affected indirectly, how the interactions affect how the change will be perceived in the organization, and how the proposed changes will affect how people carry out their work.

Figure 8 provides a way to assess and collect input about the current status versus the expected future state for each business element. Be sure to include in your conversations the potential risks and proposed actions. The point is to compare and contrast each business element to determine what is changing and the impact it will have on both the business and the people. It is less about filling out the worksheet and more about facilitating the discussion of the changes you are making. Frequently, leaders make changes to one business element and fail to consider the impact on other parts of the business ecosystem, thus setting up the initiative for ultimate failure. Therefore, discuss and capture the change impacts that need to be addressed so you can successfully implement your solution.

The more you understand the business and organization, the easier it is to identify which business elements will be

Business Impact Assessment

Business Element	Current Situation	Future State	Proposed Actions	Risks

Figure 8

impacted by the strategic initiative, who needs to be involved, and how to monitor, revise, and update your business model so that the entire business system works together.

TIP: Often companies engage management consulting firms to develop the change initiative and the business impact assessment. Whether you retain someone or do it yourself, it is imperative to use the information you have gathered so you can make informed decisions. Use the data to discuss the implications, risks, and actions to mitigate problems before you implement something that doesn't work.

Focus on the Case Study

The leaders and employees in many functional areas will ask questions about the integration. Any lack of clarity can create frustration about the nature of the combined business, including what will be merged and what will remain separate. In our case study, six weeks into the merger many departments were still working to understand the changes. Following the worksheet is a memo between the two Learning and Development departments.

Subject: Integrating Our Learning and Development Programs

To: NorthCo VP, Learning and Development

From: SouthCo VP, Learning and Development

Date: [Six Weeks after the Merger]

I was glad to get your memo and to see your thoughts about how we can start integrating our training programs. I was very interested to read through your list of training areas and courses and the curriculum summaries. I can see that our programs are quite different in terms of topics and approach, and therefore I anticipate many discussions between us and with members of the training Integration Team, as we develop our new, merged training program.

I have a few points I'd like you to start thinking about:

I see that your personnel are unionized, while ours are not. I don't know what the position of our merged company will be in relation to unions, but for now I see that your curriculum includes information and requirements from your unions. We need to discuss how this will be handled going forward.

Your curriculum summaries indicate that you focus your training on "hard skills"—what your personnel need to execute their work. While we have similar training programs, of course, we also offer optional courses on career development and "soft skills." These courses are very popular with our personnel, and I'm sure they will be with yours, too. We can talk about how to expand the course selection to meet the needs of your personnel.

For the last few years, our CEO has held an annual, two-day top leader meeting to involve more leaders in our strategy and direction. The CEO has found this to be an excellent opportunity for communicating with and grooming new leaders. Following the meeting, leaders have been assigned to strategic challenge teams to work with the CEO on aspects of our strategy. I would like to discuss ways we can continue these meetings or devise similar leadership development opportunities in which our leaders can engage directly with the CEO.

You don't mention providing financial support for your personnel when they take external courses that benefit them in their work. We are pleased to do so, as we can point to many instances when we have been able to promote people because they have acquired new skills. I'm sure your personnel will be glad to have access to this benefit, too.

I find myself talking about "your personnel" and "our personnel" but I feel sure we'll both soon be talking about "our personnel, employees of our new, merged company." I'm looking forward to helping you meet the training needs of all "our personnel."

Here is another memo, which shows how the questions about the integration can have significant impacts on the functioning and productivity of core departments.

Subject: Integrating Our Customer Service Departments

To: NorthCo VP, Customer Service

From: SouthCo VP, Customer Service

Date: [Eight Weeks after the Merger]

Great to meet you at the executive offsite meeting! I want to continue our work together as quickly as we can, because customer service has such a high priority at our company.

Let's cover a few points right now:

In comparing our customer lists, I can see that your clients tend to be larger, more established, and more function-driven than ours. Many of our customers are small or midsize companies, and many are reasonably new. We provide a high-level of service, which our customers need and appreciate. This includes doing more work for our customers—training, maintenance, etc.—than you indicate you do for your customers. For example, I see that many of your customers have their own maintenance staffs, while we often do the maintenance work for our customers, as they don't have the resources or even interest in establishing their own maintenance departments. We need to discuss how maintenance will be covered for all customers. If we stop doing the maintenance for our customers, we may lose them.

We have dedicated customer service representatives for our customers, who work alongside our sales staff. Our customers like to know who they can call directly when they need support. We train our reps in providing friendly, on-time, and responsive service. I see that you have a customer service hotline and a few reps, who are assigned to specific pieces of work; however, they are not assigned to specific customers. Our success is based on how we support our customers and provide service to them, and we need to maintain our way of doing it.

It looks to me as if your reps provide service only in response to specific requests. It is important to our customers for our reps to be proactive—providing information, dropping by now and then, sharing ideas, and so forth. This is how we interact with our customers, and they expect it, even demand it, from us.

We will clearly be selling different products into these different customers (I assume the Sales Departments are already starting to look at this), and it's not clear whether the type of customer service follows the product and customer. That is, will your reps continue to service your customers and your products, while we continue to service our customers and our products? Or will we be combining our functions into one department with one way of doing business?

This specific decision will likely be made by the Board and the CEO. In any case, I am going to push strongly for keeping our approach to providing customer service. Our customers require it, and I believe your customers will appreciate it.

Please send me your thoughts about this.

Case Study Discussion

1. What are your assumptions about the businesses and organizations in the case study? What more do you need to know?

2. How would you assess, compare, and contrast the two organizations? Use the list of core business elements in Figure 7 and capture your insights in the table below.

   How would you prioritize what needs to get done post-merger?

   Given all the complexities, how would you build agreement and alignment?

3. How do you think the NorthCo VPs from Learning and Development and from Customer Service reacted to the memos from the SouthCo VPs Learning and Development and Customer Service?

4. What do these memos tell you about how each entity runs its business?

NOTE: Here is Figure 8: Business Impact Assessment again, but this time set up for you to use in analyzing the case study. Specify how each company currently approaches the business elements. Then, for each business element, discuss the proposed actions to either merge the business or keep them separate. Determine potential risks, along with ways to mitigate the risks. Feel free to add elements and use language that applies to your business.

NorthCo and SouthCo Business Impact Assessment

Business Element	NorthCo	SouthCo	Proposed Actions	Risks

Figure 8

NOTES

Chapter 4
Understand the People and Organizational Impacts

What You Need to Know

Change initiatives often fail in execution. Why? There can be many reasons, mostly having to do with misalignment between the leaders and the employees in terms of the proposed changes. The direction may not be clear, or there is a lack of buy-in, or people lack the skills, resources, or opportunities to successfully perform their roles.

People—your human capital—are by far the best asset a company has to implement change initiatives. The organizations that can engage their people and align their work to the change initiative will achieve their goals faster and more efficiently.

With the stakes so high, you need to make sure that you "get your people-side-of-change" right:

- Do you have the right "people strategy" to implement the change?

- Is your leadership team equipped to lead the change?

- What will it take to get your leadership team and the people ready?

- What can you do right now to better leverage the discretionary effort of the leadership team and the people in the organization?

Before people are willing to make significant changes, they want to know whether it's worth putting time and effort into the new activity. They want evidence and facts that suggest the plans have a high likelihood of success. They will be assessing the level of difficulty and pondering the risk and rewards involved.

Organizational History with Change

Your organization's history dealing with previous change initiatives can positively and negatively impact how your people engage in *this* change initiative. If your people have reorganized several times in the last few years without seeing positive results, they may not readily accept yet another

---

Organizational History with Change

- What is your company or business area's past experience with change?
  - What worked/what did not work?
  - Assess your organization's history with change, including past initiatives, cross-organizational work, goal setting, implementation, leadership engagement, feedback, and results.
- Was this experience positive or negative?
- Given your organization's history with change, what actions need to be taken to prepare the organization for this change?

Figure 9

reorganization. If they have seen a revolving door of leaders in their department, people may hesitate to implement the new leader's strategy, assuming the leader will be long gone before the implementation is complete. Figure 9 provides thought-provoking questions for assessing an organization's history with change. You will use the insights you develop from answering these questions to incorporate actions into your Roadmap to build positive outcomes.

Assess Change from a People Perspective

If you want people to make a smooth transition from the current way to a new way of working, it's best to give them the opportunity to learn, understand, and prepare for these changes. In the initial stages of developing the strategic solution and change-initiative plans, analyze how the changes will affect all your different types of stakeholders. Think about these questions:

1. **Stakeholders:** Who is important in implementing this change? This may be an individual or a group of people.

2. **Changes (Behaviors):** Name the changes you will ask of others. Define the new or different actions needed from each stakeholder.

3. **Reactions and Concerns:** What kind of reactions and concerns could be encountered as you enlist the stakeholders?

4. **Impact:** How important are these stakeholder actions to the overall initiative? Assign a level of impact on the change effort—H, M, or L (for high, medium, or low).

5. Difficulty: Assign a level of difficulty—again, H, M, or L (high, medium, or low)—in getting people to perform new behaviors. An indication of high difficulty may be that you don't think a person would initiate the behavior simply by being asked to.

6. Actions: Which actions do you or others need to take to assist the individual or group? What messages and information will need to be communicated to engage people in the changes?

Figure 10 provides a worksheet to capture the people and organizational impacts. Depending on the nature and details of your change effort, you may need to modify this worksheet to meet your needs.

People and Organization Impact Assessment					
Stakeholder	Changes (Behaviors)	Reactions and Concerns	Impact (H/M/L)	Difficulty (H/M/L)	Actions

Figure 10

Focus on the Case Study

As it became clear that NorthCo was the dominant partner (almost an acquirer, and not an actual merger partner), SouthCo personnel became concerned; many were unhappy and considering leaving the company.

Memo 4

Subject: Selling into SouthCo's Marketplace

To: NorthCo SVP Sales

From: SouthCo VP Sales

Date: [Eight Weeks after the Merger]

In this memo, I am summarizing my concerns about the new sales directives:

1. Remember that our customers are mostly in the mid-market range, are cost-sensitive, and are very concerned that prices will increase. We stand to lose a significant number of our customers because our prices will be too high. So, it is crucial for us to review and reconsider the new pricing guidelines.

2. Our customers are used to high-touch customized service from us. This service has gained us customer loyalty and extended contracts. Because these mid-market customers often have smaller facilities than your larger customers, we specifically manufacture and ship smaller quantities and have historically held inventory in our warehouses. With the proposed changes, we will put much of this business at risk. If we offer a standard product line featuring your large-scale products, our customers will likely move to other suppliers.

3. Our sales processes are based on our good relationships and our problem-solving approach with our customers. Frequently, our reps become almost essential personnel for our customers, as they often know more about how our customers operate than our customers do. We do not have the same types of conversations with our customers—or prospects—as your reps do. Your sales scripts are far too formal for us, and would make our customers and prospects scratch their heads. We need to continue doing what has been successful for us.

4. For the reasons listed above, I am deeply concerned about your mandate that a NorthCo rep lead each of our selling teams. Besides the fact that we don't have your type of selling teams (we just bring our internal experts in as needed), this would send the wrong message to our reps and to our customers. Our reps pride themselves on their knowledge and relationships, and our customers rely on them for the information, service, and interactions they currently have. Our reps and customers would not understand the role of your NorthCo rep in this relationship; nor would they want to change the current relationship. SouthCo sales reps are starting to hear rumors of these changes. Several of our top salespeople have already gotten recruiting phone calls from our competitors.

Given the above, I strongly recommend that the Sales Integration Team and you think through the new directives and revise them, so that we can retain both our customer base and, frankly, our sales representatives.

Case Study Discussion

1. What are your assumptions about the people in the case study? What more do you need to know?

2. What do we know about NorthCo's and SouthCo's history with change? How will this impact the merger integration? Use the questions in Figure 9 and this table to capture your thoughts:

	NorthCo's History with Change	SouthCo's History with Change
Change History		
What Worked		
What Did Not Work		
Actions and Next Steps		

3. Based on the case study, name stakeholders impacted by this merger. Use Figure 10 to outline the changes for the people in NorthCo and SouthCo.

4. Use Figure 11 to capture and summarize the major business and people changes that will require leadership attention. After you and your team have discussed the business, people, and organizational impacts, summarize important points, implications, and actions. Then, add this information to your tools in your Toolkit. Each of these items will need to be addressed to ensure that you and your team are prepared to lead the change and that information is communicated to help your people become engaged.

Summary Implications and Actions		
Topic/Theme	**Describe Change**	**Implications**

Figure 11

NOTES

PART II

Prepare and Plan

Chapter 5

Develop Your Roadmap

What You Need to Know

Your roadmap can guide your actions and engagement with the change initiative. You should create your roadmap at the beginning of your effort and then build on and expand on it throughout the implementation.

How to Develop a Roadmap

The case for change and the business and people assessments are the starting points for crafting the roadmap. A roadmap is different from the project plan or change plan in that it captures your actions—the leader's actions—in the implementation. It helps you develop your script and action plan for leading change. Through discussions with your leadership team, you surface implementation issues and challenges and build your roadmap to engage the organization in the change activities. As the roadmap timeline is created, you are encouraged to review and identify interdependencies and conflicts with other projects and day-to-day activities.

The roadmap tool is designed to help you include the Five Keys for Leading Change in your ongoing actions. At each step in the process, you will want to review and assess how well you *and* your leadership team are doing in gaining the benefits of the Five Keys. For instance, ask yourself:

- Is my team in agreement with and alignment around the changes?

- Have people throughout the organization accepted the change?

- Are people taking action?

- Are people accepting accountability for their role in the change?

- Are all of us doing all we can to accelerate this transition to achieve the desired outcomes?

If you answer "no" to any of these questions, you should make adjustments to the roadmap to capture the missing Key(s).

TIP: If you find early success using the components of the Toolkit as a whole and the roadmap in particular, it can be tempting to celebrate an early success and abandon the approach, because you don't think you need to use the tools any longer. My clients who use this approach have said that, after they announce their strategic initiative, it felt like a "non-event." They wondered why they spent the time crafting leadership communications and creating their roadmap when it wasn't a "big issue." My experience, however, has shown that the success comes from your use of the tools, and especially the roadmap. The roadmap brings all the other components together into a timeline. The reason the initiative turned into a non-event was that these leaders were prepared and ready to handle the issues. I suggested they continue to build their roadmap to navigate the change successfully.

The whole point of using the Five Keys for Leading Change and the Toolkit is so you don't have major issues. The creation of the leadership roadmap provides a time-tested strategic thinking process, so that you create your change efforts to be "non-events." Therefore, I recommend strongly that you *not* abandon your roadmap or these tools at any point. You are gaining successes because the roadmap keeps you and your fellow leaders actively engaged in the implementation effort. This is an iterative process. Using the roadmap effectively means using it as a "live" set of plans that are built upon and adjusted as new information presents itself. As the initiative unfolds and as the result of further discussions, the roadmap will naturally need to be expanded and adjusted.

As you work through the components of the Toolkit, you should prioritize, sort, and sequence the preparations and execution of key actions across the suggested time spans. Then, leaders will know when and how to engage in the change activities. Figure 12 shows a suggested outline. The timeline helps leaders incorporate these actions into their schedules.

A Leader's Change Roadmap				
	30 Days	**60 Days**	**90 Days**	**120 Days**
Project Milestones				
Key Initiatives				
Organizational Calendar Events				
Communications Big "C"				
Communications little "c"				
Leader Actions and Preparations				
Current Projects				
Other				

Figure 12

Focus on the Case Study

The case study points to a shift in leadership intention and action as the year progressed. Initially, the two CEOs acted like equal partners and treated the merger as one of equals. The NorthCo CEO and his executives then assumed the rights of leadership, according to their preferred style. That caused people from both companies to become uneasy and feel uncertain about what was happening. The integration teams quickly devolved into NorthCo territory. Rather than merging, the two sets of executives, as well as the leaders under them, operated according to their own processes, assumptions, patterns, and culture.

Subject: Supply Chain Integration

To: MergeCo CEO (Former NorthCo CEO)

From: NorthCo VP, Procurement

Date: [Ten Weeks after the Merger]

I've been emailing back-and-forth with the person in charge of procurement at SouthCo. Some of the responses I've gotten show we have a lot of work to do to bring them up to our standard. Here are a few of the things I've picked up:

- They don't pass increased supply costs along to their customers. They claim their customers are cost-sensitive, so they simply shop around for the lowest-price suppliers.

- Because they shop around a lot, their supply chains are flexible, which means they don't have as much leverage over suppliers as we do.

- They operate on a just-in-time system, as their customers have a lot of different types of projects, and they don't want to have a lot of supplies and parts sitting in their warehouses. Think of the increased manufacturing costs involved with smaller runs and the need for express shipping.

- They don't do the data analytics we do on supply chain, so they don't know how their way of purchasing is costing them money.

Clearly, we just need to take over this function and operate the way that makes sense to us. I see a lot of potential for cost savings here.

Case Study Discussion

1. What are your assumptions about how leadership actions are planned and carried out in the case study? What more do you need to know?

2. How would the SouthCo VP, Procurement react if he saw the memo from the NorthCo VP, Procurement to the MergeCo CEO?

3. Based on what is known about the case study, how would you advise MergeCo to use the roadmap to help them with their current integration challenges?

4. Discuss how you and your team could use the concept of the leader's change roadmap (Figure 12) to lead a strategic initiative.

NOTES

Chapter 6
Communicate the Change

What You Need to Know

During times of change, people need vastly more information as well as consistency of messages. You may think you are communicating the messages sufficiently clearly that people can gain a grasp of what's going on, but this may not be true. Communication is a core leadership skill that requires constant attention. When communicating the change, consider internal and external messages, as well as the formal announcements and the informal messages delivered in groups and one-on-one conversations.

Apply Big "C"/little "c" Communications

Often, the Communications Department or Human Resources Department is enlisted to craft communications for a change effort, with a focus on the formal messages and events and the external messages, which I call the Big "C" Communications. Internal organizational announcements are typically conveyed by emails, town halls, and video conferencing. Some leaders use the external press release as their form of internal communication, which means that employees do not get the level of detail needed to do their jobs. While formal communications get the discussions started, they are not enough, because the messages are not appropriately cascaded, explained, and reinforced by the leaders.

Formal, Big "C" Communications have more impact when coupled with little "c" communications—the daily, informal group and one-on-one discussions between leaders and the people carrying out the work. One common complaint by leaders and employees alike is that the communications fail to answer questions. People see leaders having meetings, but feel left in the dark, as little information is shared with them. Effective communication requires active participation by leaders throughout the organization. This means crafting messages and preparing leaders to cascade and discuss key messages.

It's often assumed that, if the boss tells his or her direct reports something, the direct reports will know, in turn, what to communicate and how to convey the message. This can be far from the case. I see many changes fail because leaders throughout the organization weren't consistently communicating and reinforcing the formal Big "C" with the informal little "c" communications.

Whether you have a team that crafts the formal messages, or your leadership team creates the messages itself, it is prudent for you to manage *all* the messages. A strategic communications plan is a helpful tool for indicating where to get involved. Figure 13 provides a simple worksheet for you and your team to capture your communications strategy and plans. Challenge yourselves to go beyond the typical announcements and Day One launch communications to chart ongoing touchpoints within the organization. Make sure all communications are captured—both the Big "C" and the little "c" communications—and then plan to cascade and deliver consistent, timely messages.

High-Level Communications Strategy and Plan

Communication Strategy and Plan

Outline the Communication Strategy and Core Principles. How will you and your team approach communications?

1.

2.

3.

4.

5.

Capture below what needs to be communicated to the organization.

Item	Message	To Whom	Delivery (Who/How)	Timing

Brainstorm key communication touchpoints; then map them out over a timeline.

Pre-Day 1	30 Days	60 Days	90 Days	120+ Days

Figure 13

TIP: Do not assume leaders will know what to communicate and how to communicate. They get busy and often do not communicate fully. They tend to interpret the information from their own perspective. Support leaders by providing specific communications. Walk through important messages with them and discuss what and how to communicate the messages. Then, follow up to assess how the messages were received and acted upon.

Get the Messages Right

Well-crafted communications help address the physical, mental, and emotional aspects of change. Some organizations use the simple Know-Feel-Do communication concept to craft messages:

Know: What do you want people to know—the strategy, information, facts, details, steps?

Feel: What do you want people to feel? How do you want them to react when they hear the messages?

Do: What actions do you want people to take?

Many messages may cause people concern; however, if you use the right words and tone, your communication can greatly help people move to implement the change.

Communicate with the Audience in Mind

Enhance the quality of discussions by preparing ahead of time. It is easy to focus on the messages themselves and forget that the communications are intended for a specific audience. Start with the general message and create specific talking points for your key stakeholders. By creating specific messages, you can clearly communicate the message and answer anticipated questions. The Stakeholder Communication Outline in Figure 14 is a straightforward way to create individualized messages that focus on the individual or group while ensuring consistency of messaging throughout the organization.

Stakeholder Communication Outline	
Here are questions to prepare for one-on-one and group discussions with key stakeholders:	
Stakeholders	Who is important in implementing this change? This may be an individual or a group of people.
Messages	What are the messages, information, and key talking points? What are you asking this individual or group to do?
Questions and Reactions	What reactions and concerns could be encountered as you proceed? What questions can you anticipate ahead of time and be ready to answer?
Actions	What actions do you or others need to take to assist the individual or group in agreeing and aligning with the change?

Figure 14

Create a Leader Communication Toolkit

Coordinated communications start with preparing leaders at all levels to deliver the right messages. Many organizations focus on preparing executives to announce a change and assume that, once the message is delivered, the leaders will cascade the information. Instead, often the middle-level managers are left to figure out what to communicate and how to answer the numerous questions on their own. By creating a Leader Communication Toolkit, you give leaders at multiple levels the communication tools to consistently implement the messages. Figure 15 shows a checklist to develop a Leader Communication Toolkit.

Leader Communication Toolkit Checklist

☐ Leader communication instructions memo

☐ Formal organizational announcement

☐ General talking points

☐ Meeting agenda

☐ Presentation slides discussing the change, with talking points

☐ Employee handout (includes visuals and pertinent information)

☐ Frequently-asked questions for leaders

☐ Stakeholder-specific communications

☐ Communication tips

☐ Follow-on communications

☐ Ideas to collect feedback

Figure 15

TIP: Frequently, I see Leader Communication Toolkits that do not provide any more information than the formal announcement. Instead, anticipate the questions leaders will be asked and provide appropriate answers. If you want to convey different messages to various departments and functions, prepare separate Leader Communication Toolkits. When in doubt about confidentiality of information, check with your General Counsel. The key is to provide open and appropriate communications to convey messages that encourage acceptance and buy-in.

Focus on the Case Study

The case study indicates little communication was done beyond the formal announcement; the integration operated at the executive level, with no input or involvement from leaders throughout the organization. The dominant partner (NorthCo) did not have a culture of communication; little attempt was made to communicate what was happening, what should be happening, and how each employee could support the merger. As a result, NorthCo's minimalistic communication style prompted many questions in the SouthCo organization. Because SouthCo leaders were frequently tied up in meetings, they were no longer doing the regular communications and interactions that SouthCo personnel expected.

Subject: Equality, Communications, and the Merger

To: SouthCo Integration Team Lead

From: [Different] SouthCo Integration Team Lead

Date: [Ten Weeks after the Merger]

Great to catch up with you and to discuss the work on the Integration Teams. I do want to capture some of the points we discussed, as a record of our concerns about how the merger is proceeding. We've encountered the following:

- Clearly, the NorthCo people assume they are in charge. They are polite to us, but rarely really listen to what we're saying. The decisions being made are in terms of what's right for NorthCo, not MergeCo.

- Clearly, too, the NorthCo people expect that they will have the executive positions going forward. I haven't heard anything about any of our people retaining their executive positions. I assume the same will happen down through the levels of management.

- It's obvious that our carefully created and nurtured culture of openness, participation, and respect will be at least compromised, if not eliminated completely. Some NorthCo people on my team actually laughed when I told them how we work on things like transparent communications and career development with our people. I'm really upset about this.

- Along the same lines, they dismiss my comments and concerns about the lack of communication throughout the company relating to the merger. I know our people are unhappy about not knowing what's happening or what the merger means for them. We already see a drop in productivity. I'm worried that some of our key people may start to decide to leave.

- The NorthCo people do not understand how different our customers are from theirs. They seem to feel that the same manufacturing principles could be used across the board. (If this is so, can you imagine how they'll try to sell into our customer base?)

- I keep hearing that they expect our business to boost their bottom line. Profitability seems to be the only thing they expect to deliver. Don't they understand that good, solid businesses are measured and assessed on more criteria than just that?

Let's face it—this is an acquisition, not a merger. And I don't think either of us feels that all will turn out well.

Case Study Discussion

1. What are your assumptions about the communication throughout the two organizations in the case study? What more do you need to know?

2. How should the two SouthCo Integration Team Leads proceed with the work on their respective teams?

3. What actions do you advise MergeCo to take to better communicate and engage both organizations? Use the table in Figure 13 to set out a communication strategy and plan.

4. Based on what you know so far, use Figure 14 to map out communications from the MergeCo CEO to specific individuals and groups within MergeCo.

5. Outline several messages that you recommend be cascaded to the organization. Discuss how you would prepare leaders to convey consistent messages to the MergeCo organization.

NOTES

Chapter 7

Understand Your Role in Leading the Change

What You Need to Know

In any change initiative, leaders need to know and understand their roles, assess whether they are ready to lead the initiative, and figure out how to engage others. Every strategic change brings its own nuances. Whether you are new to leading change or a seasoned change leader, use the following information to facilitate discussions with your leadership team as you prepare for your role in implementing the change.

Assess Your Change Readiness

The five questions in Figure 16 will help you assess your readiness for leading change, especially for leading change in a complex situation.

Leadership Readiness Questions
1. Do you understand what's at stake?
2. Are you willing to do what it takes to make this a success?
3. How will you get others committed to and engaged in the change?
4. What do you need to do to lead this change?
5. How will you motivate yourself and others?

Figure 16

Spend some time thinking through the answers to these questions, as your answers will help you prepare to lead a successful change effort.

When you have a sense of your readiness to lead change, think about the following questions:

1. **Knowledge:** Do you know enough about the business and people to make sound decisions? Do you have pre-conceived notions about the business that could be inaccurate? What can you do to gain the knowledge required to enhance the outcomes?

2. **Relationships:** Have you built the credibility and trust throughout the organization to lead the change? Who is important to executing this change? How will you approach that and other relationships to enroll and enlist people to action?

3. **Leadership:** What worked last time may not work in this situation. Based on this current situation, what approach will you take to leading this change?

The above questions seem straightforward. Leaders usually quickly tick off that they know their businesses, have the right relationships, and have led changes before, so they feel ready and willing to lead this new effort. Unfortunately, even though many leaders assume they are ready, they are often tripped up by one or more of these three areas when trying to lead the execution of a strategic initiative.

Assess your readiness and fill in the gaps by adding key actions to your roadmap. For example, if you do not have the respect and trust of your organization, you may need to work on building the trust through sharing information and being directly involved in leading the change. Do not assume that the leadership approach you took in the last change initiative will automatically work with this change initiative. This is a different situation, so different actions are needed. Check your approach to ensure that people "want" to follow your lead. If they do, you will find yourself in a better position to accelerate the changes.

TIP: It is common for leaders to shirk their responsibilities for the change initiative. Despite the project and change management teams' efforts, the execution depends on what leaders are doing and saying to move the change from the idea to the results. The roadmap identifies the issues and lays out the plans for leaders to engage in the changes. By using the roadmap, leaders can surface issues and facilitate discussions around executing the initiative. The critical time is the handoff from the project team to the leadership, as that is when you must ensure that your leaders are ready and willing to execute the change plans.

Accelerate Behavior Change through Leader Actions

As a leader, you play an active role in encouraging people to "want" to take action and not feel like they "have to" do something. If you truly want new results, you must make sure that your actions and behaviors support the change and that your actions and behaviors cascade throughout your leadership team and the overall organization.

Figure 17 contains five change leader behaviors—things you should do—that can have a positive impact in leading change. Use these as starting points for encouraging new behaviors in others. They should become part of your roadmap.

Change Leader Behaviors

1. **Be visible and active in supporting the change.** Stay engaged and make sure you are apprised of what is going on. Walk the halls. Reach out and find out how things are progressing. Take five minutes to give your full attention to hear the answer. Check in at different sites and locations. Ask: "What's working?" "What could be improved?" "How can I help?" Listen to the answers.

2. **Communicate, communicate, communicate.** Continue to explain why the initiative is important and how people fit in. People need to hear the same messages many, many times. Every time you communicate and provide updates, act as if this is the first time you are sharing this news. Even if it's the twentieth time, communicate and answer questions. Determine how people will react to the messages. Tailor your messages, as well as the tone, language, and stories you will tell, to what the audience wants to hear, instead of what you want to tell. You will face some resistance, questions, and concerns. Identify what you can do or say that can help move people along.

3. **Demonstrate resilience.** Resilience is the ability to recover from or adjust easily to misfortune or change. Resilience allows us to find creative solutions to tricky situations. It helps us move through obstacles with ease. Resilience enables us to maintain our energy level and choose how we want to move in and out of the change implementation.

Figure 17

4. **Remove obstacles.** It is easy to get caught in a spider web of obstacles and challenges, especially with a new initiative. These obstacles can paralyze even the most motivated individuals. People need to be able to talk about where they are stuck and what they need from the leadership team to get unstuck. Leaders can help by transforming the obstacles into opportunities, breaking the problems down into smaller components, and asking people what they themselves would do to address the obstacles they are facing. By addressing the challenges head on, you can start to move people in the right direction.

5. **Provide positive and constructive feedback.** Positivity becomes contagious, feeds on itself, and leads people forward. Give positive feedback throughout the initiative, especially when you see that people are moving in the right direction. Go beyond generic expressions of "Awesome!" or "Thanks, that's great!" to provide very clear, pinpointed feedback on what you saw—and why it matters. Many leaders seem to think they don't have to give positive feedback. However, research has shown that such feedback motivates people and keeps them on course. You can also use positive feedback to overcome negatives.

Figure 17, continued

Form and Lead Your Change Management Team

One of your main roles as change leader is to form the change management team, creating one that collectively does the right things to lead the company to the results you want. You will ask your change management team to prepare and engage people in the new actions based on your change strategy. You will want the team to point out organizational changes, suggest leadership interactions, and detail implementation plans.

Remember, though, that you are the champion of the initiative, so you must be sure to review these plans and incorporate actions into your roadmap. The work of this team does not replace your work or that of your key leaders. You must remain active and visible for the change to happen, and your key leaders must play their roles, too.

Here are key ways to help your change management team gain agreement and alignment among the members:

1. **Be Clear and Focused:** Know specifically what you want your team to agree on, then focus on how you will get team members to agree.

2. **Gather the Information:** Pull together all the information needed to discuss the initiative and make a decision. This is where the case for change is useful, as long as it looks at various perspectives. Too often, a case for change is skewed to the decision a leader wants to reach and misses alternative solutions.

3. **Be Objective:** It's easy to make a decision before considering all sides of an issue. Remain objective and let go of any preconceived notions. Some participants may not speak up as readily as others. To get to the right answer, make sure that everyone's voice is heard.

4. **Make a Decision**: Determine how the ultimate decision will be made. Ensure that you have had enough conversation and have looked at different scenarios. As you start to arrive at possible options, be sure to assess the pros and cons of each. At some point, the team will be ready to make a decision. Once the decision is made, test that it holds up. Sometimes it helps to ask members of the team to explain the decision. This often surfaces different interpretations of the decision and exposes cracks in the agreement.

5. **Uphold the Decision**: The discussion can get heated, but once the decision is made, unless it is unethical or illegal, uphold it. The team should act as one voice outside the room.

TIP: Project teams and change management teams are not places for poor performers. If this is a strategic initiative expected to deliver results, put your top leaders and people on the teams.

Focus on the Case Study

The case study does not indicate a business culture or environment where change leadership actions could be carried out, or even be thought of as necessary. The flow of information was minimal; the leaders throughout MergeCo were not involved in planning the change actions. Both companies continued to try to operate as they did pre-merger, and this isn't working.

NorthCo employees may have been used to the top-down, "do-what-you're-told" approach, but SouthCo's employees were not. The emerging balance-of-power in MergeCo was noticed, but not commented on formally. There is no indication or sense that top leaders attempted to gain agreement throughout the organization to the ideas underlying the merger. SouthCo leaders were departing in large numbers, leaving former SouthCo employees without management they knew or trusted, particularly given the different cultures in the two companies.

Memo 7

Subject: Scope of Work for Our Implementation Team

To: SouthCo Division President

From: MergeCo CEO (Former NorthCo CEO)

Date: [Twelve Weeks after the Merger]

Thank you for your comments and ideas about creating a case for change.

It troubles me that people do not seem to understand that the deal is done and that we are well on our way to merging the two businesses. We all know how challenging a merger can be. People just do not like change, and it is my experience that some people will quickly self-select out of the company. Additionally, I agree: The sooner we stop talking about SouthCo and NorthCo, the sooner we can become one company and reap the benefits of the combined organization.

For the merger to be successful, we need to find significant cost savings from synergy in our operations and back office. While I understand your comments about communication and engagement, I am reluctant either to add work to our plate or to expand how this company goes about management. The former NorthCo management is very clear that this is a merger and is keen to move ahead.

What is most important for our team is setting out what needs to happen and telling the appropriate managers what they and their direct reports have to do. I have seen this process work in our company and have no doubt that it is the most streamlined and effective way for us to proceed.

The sooner we can get everyone on the same page, the sooner we will be able to grow our business. Can you put together a straw-model of a meeting to help the former SouthCo leaders get up to speed? We will review it next week.

Case Study Discussion

1. What are your assumptions about how the leaders are leading the change as shown in the case study? What more do you need to know?

2. How do you think the SouthCo Division President reacted to the response from the MergeCo CEO? What does this memo tell you about the change-leadership styles in the two companies? Which style do you think is more effective in making change happen?

3. What advice would you give the MergeCo CEO? What specific behaviors do you recommend the MergeCo leaders/managers start exhibiting to make this merger successful? How would incorporating Change Leadership Behaviors help the MergeCo leaders be more effective?

4. Discuss the Leadership Readiness Questions in Figure 16 and how the MergeCo leaders could use them to prepare to lead the integration?

NOTES

PART III

Implement

Chapter 8

Announce the Change

What You Need to Know

Organizations spend a significant amount of time turning an idea into a strategic solution. Implementing that initiative means getting others—your people—involved. It is your job to help them work through the process, so that you can successfully implement the initiative. This all starts with the announcement of the change.

The Announcement: The Call to Action

Consistency in and repetition of messages are critical to helping people process the information and move forward. It is up to you to keep messages clear and to focus your people on what they can do to support the change. Use the announcement to share both the knowns and the unknowns, and then express a call-to-action. In some cases, the call-to-action may be focusing people on the current business deliverables; in other instances, you may name specific actions to implement the solution. Use the announcement to make it clear that change is about to occur and to tell people how they can be a part of the solution.

As you prepare for the announcement, use the Communications Strategy and Plan (Figure 13) in Chapter 6, along with the Stakeholder Communication Outline (Figure 14) and Leader Communication Toolkit Checklist (Figure 15), as key inputs for the announcement and go-live activities. Figure 18 provides an Announcement Communication

Checklist to get your announcement plan started. Use this checklist to create an announcement package that communicates appropriate messages to internal and external stakeholders. Ensure that the messages get consistently communicated by developing talking points and materials

Announcement Communication Checklist

This checklist focuses on the internal communications typically cascaded by leaders. Keep separate checklists for internal and external communications, and have Communications and HR check to make sure there is consistency in the messages.

☐ General Message

☐ Email Announcement and other internal posted communications

☐ Day One Communications Plan

☐ Press Release Announcement

☐ All-Company Announcement Agenda

☐ All-Company Announcement PowerPoint and Talking Points

☐ Case for Change

☐ Leader Meeting-in-a-Box with communication messages and instructions

☐ Leader Meeting Agenda with Direct Reports

☐ External Communications Plan

☐ Customer Letter

☐ Supplier/Vendor Letter

☐ Leader FAQs

☐ Other

Figure 18

for leaders and managers to use as they cascade the information to their teams. Go beyond the announcement and provide ongoing information to help your organization begin to work in the new way.

Prepare Leaders to Cascade Messages

As you are creating the announcement communications, also create the communication plans to prepare all leaders to convey and support your messages. There is nothing worse than a leader saying, "I am learning about this at the same time as you." Employees look to their leader for information and support. Without the proper information, a leader or manager has no way of supporting the messages.

Begin your announcement communications early. This means taking into account the many discussions that occur before the announcement, so that you can enroll and enlist leaders into the plans. These initial conversations with leaders are important preparatory actions that are often ignored. Be thoughtful and prepared for these conversations to gain agreement and alignment. Use the case for change and your knowledge of the situation to craft stakeholder-specific messages that will be compelling to your leadership team.

Do not think that, if leaders were involved in developing the solution, they would all announce the strategic initiative in the same way. Create the Leader Communication Toolkit and walk through the messages and actions with your leaders. This will help them discuss the business plans, using the case for change. When leaders are aligned on the messages, they can accelerate the change. Your goal with

117

the communications is to get people to understand, agree to, and align with the initiative. You need to:

- Know what you want to communicate.

- Communicate clearly and understandably.

- Help all the leaders and managers in your organization communicate the same information repeatedly, so everyone understands and knows what to do.

- Create a regular cascade of information throughout the organization.

- Assist leaders in answering questions and addressing concerns.

- Create a mechanism to collect and address feedback from the organization.

- Use your roadmap to call out key points of leadership communication to ensure that all activities are aligned and sequenced.

Cascade communications from the C-suite down through all levels of management to the front-line supervisors, so that the formal and informal messages alike can be conveyed consistently throughout the organization. Sometimes the messages from the executives to management are the same. Other times, as messages and information are cascaded throughout the organization, more specific information and answers to questions are required. Mitigate the risk of miscommunications by creating a communication cascade, as outlined in Figure 19.

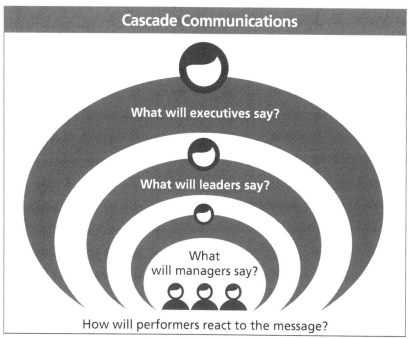

Figure 19

Use Conversations to Move to Action

The follow-on meetings and conversations are critical parts of any announcement. You can prepare leaders ahead of time to anticipate questions and concerns and to give them the tools to communicate. Set up feedback loops and a repository of information so that leaders can share reactions and review both questions and issues. Your announcement is just the beginning of the interaction. Too often, leaders announce a major strategic change, but the people hear nothing more for weeks. People may need to hear the same message several times to understand and process what is happening. This may mean communicating even when you don't think there is something new to communicate. The goal of communication is to assist others and convey information. Remember that it's all about the people to whom you are conveying the message.

Focus on the Case Study

Subject: Requests for Information

To: Former SouthCo CEO

From: SouthCo SVP Human Resources

Date: [Six Months after the Merger]

As we discussed: I've been spending a significant amount of time fielding questions from our managers—and increasingly from employees—about the status of the merger and its effects on our functions and staffing.

Our people are worried about what will be happening to their jobs. In any merger, people know there will be changes. In this merger, however, our people are sensing that there will be significant changes in their functions, processes, and jobs. They are worried. Our managers do not know what to tell their people; they themselves are uncertain about their own positions. I am hearing that some worrisome rumors about mass layoffs and demotions are circulating throughout the company.

Part of the problem is that, as our people are increasingly interacting with NorthCo personnel, they are picking up an attitude. The NorthCo people seem to be treating our people as subordinates and talking about our work and products as inferior to theirs. Our people are sensing that they will have to switch to the NorthCo way of working and doing business, and they don't like the idea of this.

We need to stabilize our workforce by communicating with them: (1) the status of the merger; (2) the plans for integration; and (3) the way they'll be working, going forward. Without these communications, I'm worried that we will start losing people. I've heard that recruiters have already started to call our top producers.

I recommend setting up a meeting of our managers, so that you can bring people up to date on what has been happening, what will be happening, and what they can tell their people.

Case Study Discussion

1. What are your assumptions about ongoing communications in the case study? What more do you need to know?

2. How should the former SouthCo CEO respond to the memo, and to the concerns outlined in it?

3. What materials and information should all NorthCo and SouthCo leaders have for working and communicating with their people?

4. If MergeCo were to announce the merger all over again, what would you recommend they do? Use the template in Figure 18 to set out a cascade of messages.

   Discuss your approach to announcement communications and outline how you would make adjustments, based on the case study details.

NOTES

Chapter 9
Keep People Engaged, Accountable, and Productive

What You Need to Know

All too frequently, after a change initiative is announced, perhaps some action takes place, but then people return to their familiar ways of conducting business. As people are the essential success factor in a change initiative, you need to find ways to keep your people engaged, accountable, and productive, if the initiative is going to succeed.

You can keep people *engaged* by focusing on short-term goals, allowing them to take action without micromanaging them, enabling them to balance their workloads to accommodate change initiative actions, and creating a culture of change in the organization.

You can instill *accountability* by giving people responsibility for actions, setting milestones against which their actions can be measured, helping them work through adversity and remove obstacles, and generally creating a culture of commitment and caring throughout the organization.

You can build *productivity* by focusing people on the work to be done, making sure they see the progress resulting from their actions, minimizing disruptions and interruptions, and ensuring that they know which are the most important tasks that need to be accomplished.

Clearly, setting goals and expectations helps people understand how their leaders are defining accountability and productivity. Monitoring actions and working to shape behaviors are essential to involving people in the change and making them feel their actions are useful and productive.

Cultivate New Behaviors

One of the challenges in leading change is that leaders need to find quick ways to change behaviors and actions, so that people can start working in a new way. The most common, and least successful, way is to "tell" someone what to do and assume they will do it. In times of change, people may desire the outcomes of change, but may be reluctant, uncomfortable, or not at all interested in adjusting what they are doing. So how can leaders efficiently engage people in a new way? I suggest defining what needs to be done—that is, identifying which new behaviors would lead to results and which could get in the way.

The classic way to analyze behavior is known as an "ABC Analysis." This analysis is based on B. F. Skinner's work on applied behavior science, not the ABC Analysis attributed to Pareto Analysis in inventory management nor the ABC cost accounting tool. In this case, we are talking about how to identify critical behaviors that may not naturally happen by "telling" someone or training the person in what to do.

The "A" in "ABC" stands for *antecedent*. An antecedent is something that triggers or prompts the behavior. A message from the boss asking for a report or an email with a request for data are antecedents.

The "B" stands for *behavior*, which is defined as what someone says or does. You will want to get very specific about the behavior you want to develop.

The "C" stands for a *consequence* to the person performing the behavior. It is the response to the behavior after the performer's behavior has occurred. For example, the consequence may be criticism from the boss, which could result in the employee's not wanting to try that action again. Or it may be positive feedback from the boss, in which case the employee will likely try this action—the behavior—again. After giving a presentation, a presenter may be asked to follow-up on specific actions. Depending on the presenter, the request could be considered a welcome consequence or may be considered additional work to their busy schedule.

In times of change, we ask people to step out of their comfort zone and try new behaviors. Most changes require people to stop doing what they are currently doing and start doing something new. To prompt new behavior, it helps to identify the antecedents or prompts to get the new behavior started. Telling people what to do is not always enough. To keep people working in new ways and forming new habits often requires both positive reinforcement and encouragement. Leaders can play a significant role in accelerating the change by providing coaching and feedback to keep people working in the new way. When people get stuck, it helps when leaders are available to answer questions and remove the obstacles in the way of progress. Figure 20 provides a visual of the cascade of behaviors from leaders to individual performers. It helps to capture critical new behaviors that may not naturally occur without the appropriate prompts and positive consequences from leadership interactions.

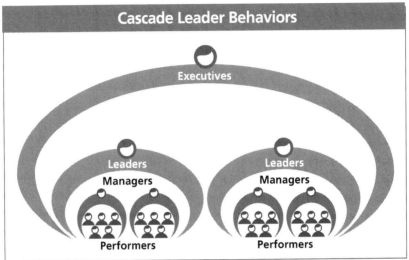

Figure 20

TIP: Whenever you ask people to perform new behaviors that are critical to the success of your initiative, assess whether these behaviors will occur naturally after you request a specific action. Often, getting new behaviors started requires the right antecedents, and particularly the right positive reinforcement.

The Power of Positive Reinforcement

As leaders, we can play a significant role in providing positive reinforcement to increase new behaviors. Too many change efforts focus on simply the prompts—those triggers that get new behaviors started—such as training, instructions, and job aids. However, the real power of accelerating behavior change comes through positive reinforcement, including positive feedback, recognition, and ongoing support.

It is amazing how people "want" to contribute to the overall success of the business if they know the leader is paying attention. As human beings, we are often conditioned to repeat behaviors that are reinforcing to us when we receive positive feedback. Typically, people in a work setting will shy away from and avoid anything that may feel negative or punishing to them. When leaders say nothing or criticize and ridicule a project, it can suck the life out of the effort. Your actions can have a huge impact in encouraging or shutting down new actions.

Leaders can play a very active role in providing frequent, feedback to accelerate behavior change. With a positive change in behavior, the results will follow.

Your roadmap should include the new behaviors required to support the change—that is, the behaviors needed to initiate the work. Additionally, you and your leadership team should discuss how you will use consequences to convert new behaviors into habits by liberally providing positive reinforcers. These reinforcers include things like providing positive feedback, removing challenges, discussing options to solve problems, collaborating, and making decisions.

Cascade Behaviors through Leader Actions

When a change is announced, people typically attend communication and training sessions to learn about the new approach. These sessions, while an effective way to orient people to the new situation, are usually not enough for people to start working in the new way. They can be terrific prompts, but information needs to be turned into action. Action comes from the application of the training and information.

Leaders are in a unique position to reinforce new actions in real time in the workplace. Here are steps for developing a behavioral cascade, ranging from defining the actions of individual performers to guiding the actions of executives and the leadership:

- Define the desired behaviors. Name the behaviors that may be difficult to implement and maintain but that are critical to the success of the effort. Pick a few.

- Express each behavior, using action words. Be as specific as possible, since vague phrases can be subjective and confusing.

- Create the leadership behavior cascade. Develop behavior-shaping plans. Begin with the individual performer's behavior, and then determine what leaders at each level need to do and say to support the new behavior. Write out your actions as well as those of the appropriate members of your leadership team that will be needed to support these new behaviors. What will people require from the leadership team to keep this behavior going? The Change Leader Behaviors outlined in Figure 17 can help you provide positive reinforcement to encourage the new behaviors.

- Incorporate these actions into your roadmap.

- Ask leaders to observe, coach, and give feedback to their direct reports when they see someone execute the defined behavior.

- Gather feedback and discuss the progress. Understand what's working and what can be improved on.

- Celebrate even the smallest progress. Spread positive news and stories about the implementation successes.

By developing the behavior cascade from the individual performer up through the senior leaders, you can get everyone aligned and committed to doing the new actions and accelerating the change. Figure 20 shows a cascade of leader behavior aimed at providing support to performers working on new activities. Figure 21 outlines an example of a behavior-shaping plan with the intent of ensuring positive results through behavior change.

Behavior-Shaping Plan

○ **Executive Actions**	What can executives do to support the new behavior?
○○ **Leader Actions**	What can leaders do to reinforce this new behavior?
○○○○ **Manager Actions**	What can managers do to reinforce this new behavior?
○○○○○○ ○○○○○○ **Performer Actions**	What is the desired behavior?

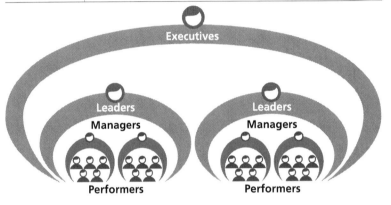

Example

○ **Executive Actions**	• *Communicate how sales projection accuracy enhances the business results.* • *Identify and remove obstacles to enhance sales projections.* • *Give positive feedback and acknowledge those who consistently input accurate sales projections.*
○○ **Leader Actions**	• *Discuss sales projections with managers in one-on-ones.* • *Discuss sales projection summary in management meetings.* • *Point out employees with top results.*
○○○○ **Manager Actions**	• *Review sales projection of each account rep. and provide suggestions.* • *Provide weekly positive and constructive feedback to account reps..*
○○○○○○ ○○○○○○ **Performer Desired Behavior**	• *Input accurate sales projections at the end of the day.*

Figure 21

Build a Culture of Accountability

Accountability is a broad set of behaviors. In organizations where people feel accountable, they have a sense of ownership of their work. Organizations that support a culture of ownership will typically create a safe environment for people to try new approaches that may succeed or even fail. Accountable cultures start with establishing transparent and clear communications, building trust, and respecting others.

Below are 10 suggestions to build accountability for the change effort. Use this list to come up with how your organization will approach accountability:

1. Lead by example—be a role model of accountability.

2. Operate with honesty and integrity. Be clear about what is nonnegotiable, so that people are not surprised.

3. Build trust by being straightforward, transparent, and thoughtful in how you communicate and engage people in change. Cultivate trust by acknowledging the work of others.

4. Set mutual expectations. Work collaboratively, using goals, metrics, and plans.

5. Define the span of accountability and control, so that people know where decisions are made and how to work with one another.

6. Share successes and own the failures.

7. Give people choices—create a culture that cares what people think. Let people have a voice and input into the work product.

8. Use the power of feedback to give people the knowledge and insights to enhance future actions.

9. Smooth out the bumps and hiccups by offering resources and removing impediments.

10. Make accountability an expected way of operating.

Focus on the Case Study

In mergers-and-acquisitions, people are asked to change what they are currently doing, so as to act differently in the combined entity. The memos and situations posed throughout these chapters are laying out many instances where the actions of NorthCo and SouthCo are quite contradictory. It will take significant behavior change in both companies for them to operate as a merged company. Thus far, the leadership has neither addressed nor defined the behaviors that need to change.

Memo 9

Subject: Staffing Priorities

To: NorthCo, VP Human Resources

From: MergeCo (formerly NorthCo) Distribution Manager

Date: [Eight Months after the Merger]

As you know, two months ago, I became the MergeCo Manager of the Distribution Operations across all our locations. As directed by the Integration Team, I have told all locations to use our standard forms and processes, and I'm making sure each location has personnel who know how we do distribution.

I'm running into some problems:

- SouthCo personnel have complained that it takes too long to fill out the forms, the computer doesn't allow them to advance to the next screen, and the information isn't relevant to their business. When I spoke with the distribution supervisors, they said they would take care of it, but that was weeks ago. I am seeing real differences in how the two companies handle things.

- There's a lot of turnover in the SouthCo locations. In some locations, we're down to half the people we need. I know we're not supposed to do any hiring, but how are my supervisors to get the products to the customers, without paying a lot of overtime?

- SouthCo had distribution people working with specific customers. These people don't like it when the supervisor sends a different crew to what they see as their customer. There's a lot of complaining, and I also don't think people are working as hard as they could.

I don't know how I'm supposed to maintain a smooth-running distribution operation if my supervisors and I can't control how the work gets done. I need to take action to get the people with the right attitudes in place.

Case Study Discussion

1. What are your assumptions about how leaders are keeping people engaged, accountable, and productive in the case study?

2. How do you think the NorthCo VP, Human Resources will react and respond to the memo?

3. What would you suggest that leaders, managers, and supervisors do to get their people to use the standard forms? Use the worksheet in Figure 21 to create a Behavior-Shaping Plan.

4. What recommendations would you make to MergeCo to build accountability in its organization?

5. What can MergeCo do to improve productivity of its people?

NOTES

Chapter 10

Manage Resistances

What You Need to Know

Change impacts people in a variety of ways—physically, emotionally, mentally, and even spiritually. When individuals hear there will be change, they may wonder:

- What's going to happen to me?

- Is this a significant change or a small one?

- How will this affect my work?

- Will this change negatively impact me?

- Will my efforts be valued?

- What should I do about the change?

- Is my job in jeopardy?

- What's in it for me?

- Whom can I trust?

Move People from Resistance to Action

Your change initiative may be derailed by resistance from personnel at all levels in the organization. People may resist because they don't feel they know what's happening or can't see what's in the change for them. These people may share their concerns with coworkers, spreading the resistance, especially in the absence of information and communications.

To successfully drive change, leaders must think in terms of moving people from resistance to acceptance to action. This is where a clear case for change is essential for consistently communicating the messages. Use the case for change to enlist people to participate in the change.

Without clear direction, people are left wondering what to do. You must play an active role in observing and monitoring what is going on and in answering people's questions. It is always good to acknowledge specific concerns and help people understand what the change means for them. Your goal is to make people feel that they are part of the change and the solution and that they are working with you to create the future of the company.

Overcome Resistance

People resist change for many reasons:

- They think change signals loss for them.

- They didn't see the change coming.

- They don't believe the change is necessary or will succeed.

- They weren't involved in the decision.

- They don't see clear outcomes.

- They don't see a compelling enough reason to make the change.

- They don't think this is a great time to launch yet another initiative.

- They think the change may benefit the business, but not them.

- They think everything is fine the way it is.

You and your leadership team can be positioned to anticipate and mitigate the natural resistance. Instead of letting resistance fester, act. Name the resistance. Identify ways to mitigate it by addressing and removing the objections. Help people focus on what is under their own control and what small actions they can take to move in the right direction. You do not need to have all the answers; ask people what *they* can do to move to accept the new way and take positive action. Provide people with a positive action they can take. Figure 22 provides a mechanism for naming and handling the resistances that surface.

TIP: Resistance and objections may not be logical. When someone expresses an objection or reaction to a change, we are taught to respond rationally and logically. However, when it is an emotional objection, no amount of logic or facts will help. In fact, people may even push back on your logic. So, what can you do to help someone get unstuck? Start by acknowledging the issue and step into the conversation. Let the person process and talk through their perspective. Listen to the person's objection without defending the solution. Listen carefully and identify the objection. Can you figure out the underlying concern or fear? Paraphrase and reframe the objection, using stories, metaphors, and analogies. Support your stories with proof and facts. Finally, work on next steps and expectations.

Handling Resistance

Name the Resistance	Ways to Move to Acceptance and Action

Leader	Individual	Observations	What I Need from You

Figure 22

Focus on the Case Study

The case study is clear about NorthCo and SouthCo having different cultures, operating in different environments and marketplaces, and having different leadership styles. As it became clear that NorthCo was the dominant partner (almost an acquirer and not a merger partner), SouthCo personnel began to leave (perhaps the most expressive form of resistance an employee can take).

Memo 10

Subject: Staff Turnover

To: SouthCo SVP, Human Resources

From: SouthCo Functional Manager

Date: [Nine Months after the Merger]

I want to let you know why I haven't submitted my quarterly HR update. Basically, I'm having a lot of problems with our personnel. People are spending a significant amount of time complaining. In the past 3 months, I've lost 5 people, including my top 2 supervisors, and I can tell that more people are ready to leave. You know their reasons: lack of information, uncertainty about their jobs, the attitudes of the NorthCo people we must deal with, and not knowing how they'll be integrating with the NorthCo people. When I spoke with my NorthCo counterpart, he says these are all to be expected in an acquisition.

People feel like they are in the dark and say they are very frustrated with the lack of direction. I am trying my hardest to keep people focused on what they can influence, but they are expecting the worst. I'm worried that I could have some workplace conflicts, and I don't know how to handle this situation. (As you know, I'm having my own problems working with the NorthCo people!)

I doubt I'm the only one facing these issues. If you have any ideas about how to handle the situation, let me know. Meanwhile, with this as background, I'll send you my report.

Case Study Discussion

1. What are your assumptions about the resistances you see in the case study? What more do you need to know?

2. As the SouthCo SVP, Human Resources, how would you respond to the memo from the SouthCo Functional Manager?

3. What can the Functional Manager do about mitigating the resistance and turnover? Set out plans for dealing with the various types of resistance, using the tables in Figure 22.

4. From what you know having read the case study, name other resistances and ways in which MergeCo could help people move to acceptance and action.

NOTES

Chapter 11
Monitor and Measure Progress

What You Need to Know

Using Data to Your Advantage

As you and your organization implement the change initiative, you will want to monitor and measure your progress to determine whether you are getting the results required to meet your goals. Most organizations do this work by collecting data and reporting it on dashboards. Dashboards, whether they be a simple spreadsheet or electronic software programs, are a handy tool to provide an at-a-glance progress report of key performance indicators (KPIs) of a change initiative. Here are a few points to keep in mind about data collection and the use of dashboards:

- Your data collection and monitoring should involve both quantitative and qualitative measurements. Too many organizations focus solely on quantitative data.

- You can use the data you have collected as a learning opportunity—for you, your leaders, and the entire organization. Your collection and analysis of data can be used to support your people, give positive and constructive feedback, and coach your people through the change.

- Your collection and use of the data should reinforce actions and behavior. You should communicate throughout the organization that you will *not* be using the data to criticize and blame, but rather to keep the initiative and the behavioral changes on track.

- You should collect the qualitative data that can be used to determine whether your people are working in the new ways that will lead to the results.

- Your data collection should involve multiple types of actions: listening, observing, following the behaviors, and probing the engagement of the management team.

- Remember that dashboards are backward-looking. If the change initiative is strategic to your business, find early indicators of progress, which you can get through real-time observations and reporting.

Building a Measurement Culture to Drive Results

When you measure progress toward results, everyone can stay on top of the goals. Unfortunately, some leaders use measurements only when an initiative is failing. Or they track solely high-level results, which makes it difficult for people to understand how their own actions played a role in those results when they're told about them.

Measuring progress works best when you establish a culture of measurement throughout the company. The process of measurement can then be used to drive the behavior you want to see. You can build a management culture by:

- Setting realistic targets

- Cascading measurements throughout the organization. (A cascade of measurements involves establishing measurements at all levels in the organization, so that everyone can be held accountable for actions, contributions, and results.)

- Failing fast and moving on

- Shaping adoption and action by driving measurement throughout the organization

- Creating transparency around the measurements

- Monitoring the changes longer than you planned

- Celebrating small wins throughout the initiative

- Capturing lessons learned by measuring progress and results

Using Measurement to Sustain Change

The dashboard you design should match the data collection and tracking you are doing for each particular change initiative. You need not use the same dashboard for each initiative. The dashboard should also match your measurement culture, supporting the actions you and your leaders will take in relation to the data. Figure 23 presents questions you can use to build your dashboard.

Measurement Dashboard Questions

- Which leading indicators are you measuring? What signs will you look for that people are working in the new way?

- Are the measurements a realistic representation of progress toward the goals?

- Who is involved in the measurements?

- How do your milestones and benchmarks translate into short-term goals for people to use to monitor their own progress?

- How will you use the measurements?

- How will you collect and measure your people's measurements?

- What is the data telling you?

- Do you need to adjust the measurements to match the goals and milestones?

Figure 23

Focus on the Case Study

Here are two memos related to monitoring and measuring in the case study. The first looks at process issues. The second deals with goal setting and the use of goals in measuring.

The case study indicates that the two CEOs operated separately and that responsibility for implementing the change initiative was spread across as many as 50 implementation teams. The case study does not talk about agreement around goals, benchmarks/milestones, or steps of progress; the only talk of goals was at the top level, covering potential synergies and cost savings, without mention of how these goals would be achieved. People were left in the dark about the merger. Behind the scenes, people struggled with trying to figure out what to do. As a result, productivity dropped, people were refusing to implement the changes, and the integration activities were stalled from the top of the organization all the way down to the shop floor. Meanwhile, employees, the post-merger Board, and the larger business community all sensed that the merger was not producing results and that MergeCo had no means of identifying, monitoring, and assessing where any progress at all was being made.

Memo 11

Subject: Integration Progress

To: MergeCo CEO (Former NorthCo CEO)

From: Project Integration Leader

Date: [Ten Months after the Merger]

I will have the progress report on your desk by Friday. The report will not show the progress you want, because we're running into a serious issue: The SouthCo people, both on the Integration Team and down through management, act as if they're still reporting to the SouthCo CEO and are doing the same work, producing the same products, and using the same processes as before the merger. It's as if a merger hasn't happened.

Any progress being made involves our Integration Team Members trying to set the processes we'll be using, going forward. We're ready to get the processes in place, but the SouthCo people keep talking about needing to see the milestones and benchmarks that will tell them the new processes are working properly. They keep asking "Why?"—why we need this process, why this process has to be uniform across all locations, why they should even use this process when their CEO wants them to keep working as they have been. I thought the SouthCo CEO was championing this integration; however, I am having a tough time getting him involved. Our conversations revert to complaints by SouthCo people regarding all the changes imposed on SouthCo.

I really need your help here. Can you and the Board work to get consensus around top leadership, so the SouthCo people can understand their "Whys?" and so my integration teams can give you the results you want? It would really help if everyone could hear from you about where we are headed. People are not listening to me.

Case Study Discussion

1. How should the MergeCo CEO respond to this memo?

2. What do the MergeCo CEO and Board need to do to set
   MergeCo on the path of progress?

3. What tools do you recommend that MergeCo use to monitor
   and assess progress? Discuss which leading indicators MergeCo
   could look for as signs that people are accepting the merger.

The case study does not talk about agreement around goals, benchmarks, milestones, or steps of progress. Rather, the only talk of
goals was at the top level, covering potential synergies and cost
savings, without mention of how these goals would be achieved.
Pre-merger, the two companies measured progress in different
ways according to their cultural and marketplace factors, using
different quantitative and qualitative measures to track progress
and success in generating results.

Subject: Implementation Team Goals

To: MergeCo CEO (Former NorthCo CEO)

From: NorthCo Integration Team Leader

Date: [Ten Months after the Merger]

I will have the progress report on your desk by Friday. I must tell you, though, that the report will *not* show the progress you want. I am not alone in having difficulties getting the SouthCo people to:

- Participate in team meetings

- Participate in our goal-setting sessions

- Agree to and adopt our measurement processes in their facilities

- Understand the corrective actions we need to take when the measurements do not show the results you want

Basically, what we're seeing from SouthCo tells us that we need to accelerate taking over the management of all SouthCo operations, so that we can get them to work and produce as we need them to do. You and I have talked, over the years, about the need for "aggressive" goals and numbers, and that's what we have to set for them. When they know what's expected, they will likely start working to meet what we need.

My fellow Integration Team Leaders and I want to meet with you to set a schedule for accomplishing this work.

Case Study Discussion

1. What are your assumptions about the milestones, benchmarks, and goals in the case study? What more do you need to know?

2. How do you think the MergeCo CEO will react to the memo from the NorthCo Integration Team Leader? How do you think the SouthCo members of that Integration Team would react to the memo?

3. What do you recommend that MergeCo do to measure the progress and results? Use the questions in Figure 23 to guide your discussion. How should MergeCo communicate the progress to the organization?

NOTES

Chapter 12
Accelerate the Change

What You Need to Know

Throughout this book, I have been talking about the things leaders can and should do to make change happen. Implicit in everything I have been saying is that, for leaders to make change happen, they need to make sure all parts of the initiative are happening on schedule, and act to get their leadership team and employees working on their parts of the change in a timely fashion.

This means that you need to keep it moving forward—and even accelerate the change. This requires planning, managing the handoff from project team to leaders, and monitoring what is happening.

Two leadership tools are especially important to keeping change initiatives moving forward: the Five Keys for Leading Change, and the Toolkit.

The Five Keys for Leading Change

The Five Keys for Leading Change (which you have been using throughout this book) offer an effective way to assess the change initiative and determine whether it is moving forward as efficiently as possible. Addressing these Five Keys is indeed essential to implementing—and even accelerating—your change initiative. These Keys help you lead yourself *and* your people, since, as you know by now, your people are critical assets in making change happen.

157

To review, the Five Keys for Leading Change are:

1. **Accountability.** People must acknowledge that the change is necessary and that they own their part in making the change happen. Look for early adopters who are committed to the change and are starting to deliver results.

2. **Agreement & Alignment.** The leadership team must reach agreement about the change, why it is important, and how success will be measured. Then it is necessary for people to align themselves and their actions with the change.

3. **Acceptance.** People must accept the need for change as quickly as possible, so that they can become active in the change. If people struggle to accept the change, your organization will not get behind the effort.

4. **Actions.** You must demonstrate through your own actions how you want your people to behave. People become more willing to carry out their parts in the change initiative if they understand what's in it for them, how the initiative affects them, and how their own work impacts the overall initiative.

5. **Acceleration.** You can increase the likelihood of success, if you pay attention to building a change culture, by reinforcing the actions needed to effect change.

Engage *all* your people in the implementation and encourage them as they carry out their work. See Appendix A for more information on how you can use the components of the Toolkit to apply the Five Keys to your change initiative.

Another Look at the Toolkit

We have discussed how to use the components that make up your Toolkit to create plans to lead your change effort. The Toolkit gives a structure to work though the critical change components. These components help you to identify the actions you and your leaders should take to make the implementation successful.

A leader's goal in leading change is to provide the information and conditions to get people throughout the organization to agree to the change, align their work with the new processes and systems, accept what is happening, and take the actions (often both new actions and new behaviors) to support the change. When leaders can gain commitment and ownership of the change, the initiative builds momentum toward achieving the desired outcomes.

The table in Figure 24 presents a suggested set of activities that lay out the Toolkit components over a timeline in terms of Setting the Context, Preparing and Planning the Execution of the Initiative, and Implementing the changes.

The power of using the components of the Toolkit lies in the leader discussions and decisions that you and your team make. The components of the Toolkit come together into a roadmap that provides the structure for leaders to think, strategize, plan, and take action. The roadmap allows leaders to know what to do and how to show up to lead the organization forward. It provides both the discipline and the flexibility to make adjustments without losing any vital components.

Toolkit Timeline Activities

Inputs	Set the Context	Prepare and Plan
• Business Concept	• Translate Business Plan into a Case for Change	• Develop Communication Strategy & Plan
• Strategy and Business Plan	• Gain agreement and alignment with Executive Team	• Agree on Leadership Role
• The Solution, System, Process, Initiative	• Assess Business Impacts	• Create Behavior-Shaping Plans
• Project Plan	• Understand People and Organizational Impacts	• Address Interdependencies
• Change Management Plan	• Review Organizational History with Change	• Anticipate Resistance & Roadblocks
	• Summarize Implications and Actions	• Set up Measurement & Feedback Systems
	• Reconfirm Executive Agreement and Alignment	• Craft General & Stakeholder Messages
	• Draft the Roadmap	• Map out Announcement Communications
	• Outline Metrics Dashboard	• Develop External Messages
		• Construct Leader Communication Toolkit
		• Prepare Leadership to Communicate and Lead
		• Develop Roadmap Timeline
		• Check the 5 Keys and Adjust

Implement		
Announcement/Day One	**Implementation**	**Making Progress**
• Formal Announcement	• Engagement Work Sessions	• Monitor Progress
• Cascade messages and informal conversations	• Leader Cascade to Shape New Behaviors	• Reinforce New Behaviors
• Hold Department and Functional Meetings	• Ongoing Communications	• Celebrate successes and quick wins
• Gather feedback	• Executive Review Sessions	• Capture Lessons Learned
• Provide training, tools, and support	• Reinforce New Behaviors	• Link to Next Initiative
• Roadshows & Townhalls	• Monitor and Assess Progress	
• Follow up and Feedback	• Measure Results	
• Implement "Must Have" Actions	• Remove Obstacles	
• Plan Ongoing Communication	• Review and Adjust Roadmap Timeline	
• Check the 5 Keys and Adjust	• Check the Five Keys and Adjust	
	• Celebrate small wins	

Figure 24

Focus on the Case Study

The case study indicates that the two CEOs knew they had to work quickly, and that if they did not make significant progress in merging within one year, they may lose the opportunities they wanted to create. The establishment of 50 implementation teams suggests that the leaders know that business processes and practices needed to be handled quickly, and all at the same time. The implementation teams focused on processes and business matters. There is no guidance to the implementation teams on how to incorporate the people aspects of their changes. The case study does not indicate whether any implementation teams were established to handle the people and cultural aspects, beyond the functional human resource organizational design, benefits, and compensation. While the two CEOs knew these aspects were important, there appeared to be a gap between knowing and doing.

Subject: Drop of MergeCo's Stock Price

From: MergeCo CEO (Former NorthCo CEO)

To: Implementation Team Leaders

Date: [One Year after the Merger]

In today's Board of Directors meeting, a number of directors raised concerns about the drop in MergeCo's stock price. Some blame the drop on the business press's negative reporting about the slow pace of integration; others blame the drop on the lack of cost savings from integrating similar functions.

The Board has asked me to prepare a report that (1) explains for each functional area why the integration is delayed, and (2) sets out in each functional area the anticipated cost savings over the coming six months. I need from each of you your assessment of why your integration activities are not yet complete and your plan for reaching your financial targets. Include pertinent supporting data and your schedule for meeting your financial goals. Because my report must be distributed before next month's Board meeting, please submit your input to me by the end of this week.

Clearly, we need to prioritize the actions that will deliver the results we need. Your input will be used to identify those actions and to set quantitative goals for making progress in your area.

Case Study Discussion

1. Select one functional area. Draft a top-level assessment for the CEO of why the integration in a functional area you select is behind schedule. Use the case study and your own assumptions to draft a report. Be sure to address the leadership aspects in the report.

2. What advice would you give the MergeCo CEO on how to turn around the integration activities and put the business on a path to success? Discuss how the tools in the Toolkit could help MergeCo refocus and revitalize the integration activities.

3. What recommendations do you have for MergeCo for leading the integration?

Unfortunately, MergeCo did not adequately prepare for the merger integration. What was intended to be an opportunity for both companies became a disaster for MergeCo, its employees, its shareholders, and its customers. Appendix B lays out the rest of the MergeCo story, as well as how the company could have avoided the integration challenges.

Appendices C and D provide two additional case studies that share details on how the Five Keys and the Toolkit components were instrumental in the success of their respective change efforts.

You can find additional resources and free downloads on our website, **www.hapgrp.com**, under "Resources."

May you find a way to bring out your best self in leading yourself and others through these changing times!

NOTES

Appendices

Working with the Five Keys for Leading Change

When the change impacts what people are doing, leaders will require tools and techniques to quickly get people working in the new way. The Five Keys for Leading Change are a lens for leaders to use to strategize, plan, and execute the strategic initiative, while engaging an organization that may not readily accept and adopt the changes. The Five Keys and the Toolkit approach give leaders a set of change techniques they can easily utilize in conversations to gain agreement and alignment and to ensure positive actions.

As the leader, you likely do not need to take all the actions yourself; however, you *will* want to make sure the right actions are happening to make the change successful. There is nothing worse than a brilliant plan stalled at one or two levels of leadership because the leaders have not thoroughly agreed to nor taken the time to get aligned with the endeavor. You will want to stay highly engaged for several reasons. First, people will follow your lead; if you are engaged, they should be engaged, too. Second, you will see first-hand how actions are affecting the implementation and outcomes. Finally, you will have an opportunity to provide direct feedback and input to shape the way forward. If you want results quickly, then my advice is to ensure that you and your leadership team are engaged to make it happen.

Throughout this book we have discussed how to incorporate the Five Keys (Figure 2) and the components of the Toolkit (Figure 3) to support you in uncovering and resolving the issues, particularly the people aspects of change. In this appendix, I provide an outline of the kinds of questions and topics that can help you facilitate the discussions with your leadership. As I've mentioned, it is not filling out forms that matters, but rather conducting all the conversations, decisions, and execution of the plans that makes the difference between leadership teams that succeed and those that fail.

The following material summarizes the components of the Toolkit and suggests discussion questions and ways to incorporate the Five Keys to execute a change effort.

1. Collect the Inputs

Collect the information regarding the strategic initiative and assess the changes you are asking the organization to make to drive new outcomes.

- Do you have a clear picture regarding the strategy and goals of your initiative and other projects?

- Is there agreement on the concept or solution?

- Is the strategy or solution ready to implement, or will you be asking the organization to develop them in the implementation plan?

- Has the leadership team talked about and assessed the risks and rewards associated with embarking on this change?

- Is the leadership team willing to lead the changes with and through people in the organization? See questions in Figure 16.

- With which of the Five Keys for Leading Change may you and your organization struggle as you execute your change initiative?

2. Define the Case for Change

Translate the business strategy and plans into terms that people can relate to and can then take action.

- How will you convert your business plan or solution into a set of messages that people understand? See Figure 5 for discussion questions.

- How will you articulate these changes so that people understand? What is the compelling reason that people will "want" to engage in these changes— "what's in it for them?"

- Which Keys are essential for the case for change to be compelling to your stakeholders?

- How will you measure success both quantitatively and qualitatively? What evidence will you expect to see if the initiative is on track?

3. Assess the Business Impacts

A strategic change in one business element usually affects other business elements. When business elements are not aligned, they create inconsistency in organizational messaging and difficulty carrying out the work; then results fall short. Facilitate a discussion about the proposed business element changes.

- Determine how this strategic change fits within the other business elements. Use the list of business elements in Figure 7 and others relevant to your business to assess, compare, and contrast the current situation and the desired end result. Capture your insights in Figure 8.

- Given all the complexities and other organizational activities, prioritize what needs to be done to make all your work activities successful. How would you build agreement and alignment? Outline plans to address the business elements so that people stay engaged and work flows smoothly.

- Based on the business element adjustments, which of the Five Keys will you and your team need to consider as you implement the solution?

NOTE: This is not a check-the-box exercise. It's meant to surface inconsistencies in the changes proposed, versus the current business model. Go beyond an assessment of the business elements and discuss the challenges, obstacles, and risks. Develop ways to mitigate any risk so that your changes work within the business model and have an opportunity to succeed. There may be obvious inconsistencies between business elements, and sometimes very subtle shifts can cause problems down the road if not addressed.

4. Assess the People and Organizational Impacts

With the stakes so high, you need to make sure that you "get the people-side-of-change right." Once you have identified the business changes, then work through how these changes affect various stakeholder groups. This enables you to create the appropriate engagement plans, using the Five Keys as a guide.

- Discuss your organization's history with change. Use the questions in Figure 9 to guide the conversation. Capture learnings and areas to pay attention to as you develop communications and other engagement plans.

- Based on your situation, name stakeholders affected by this change. Use Figure 10 to outline the changes by stakeholder group.

- Use Figure 11 to capture and summarize the major business and people changes that will require leadership attention. After you and your team have discussed the business, people, and organizational impacts, summarize important points, implications, and actions to be added to your leadership change roadmap. Each of these items will need to be addressed to ensure that you and your team are prepared to lead the change and that information is communicated sufficiently clearly to help people become engaged.

- Have you addressed the Five Keys to engage people in the change? What do you and your team need to do to address the objections and remove the obstacles to assist people in working in the new way?

- Discuss how the actions you surface address the Five Keys for Leading Change.

5. Communicate the Change

Communications go far beyond the formal announcement. Messages are reinforced in the informal discussions. People take direction from their direct manager. Therefore, if the messages are inconsistent, the changes will not be fully realized.

- Create your communication strategy and core communication principles so that everyone communicates consistent messages. See Figure 13 for an outline of a communication strategy.

- Lay out the formal communication touchpoints. Make sure that the formal communications and informal conversations, the one-on-ones, and the small group discussions appropriately cascade the messages to move people from understanding to acceptance to action. Figure 14 provides a useful way to capture and sequence specific stakeholder messages.

- Take note of other initiatives occurring simultaneously and ensure that there is clarity of expectations. There is nothing worse than a communication debacle because of conflicting messages.

- Prepare leaders to cascade messages using the Leader Communication Toolkit Checklist in Figure 15.

- Craft announcement communications using Figures 18 and 19 as guides to capturing your messages. Incorporate these communication activities into the roadmap.

- How will you and your leadership ensure that the Five Keys for Leading Change are addressed in your communications?

6. Lead the Change

Executing change takes more than the strategy and plans. To accelerate the change and to manage the complexity of constant changes requires consistent leadership actions throughout the organization to keep the initiative on track. Get prepared to lead change using the questions in Figure 16 to assess your change readiness.

- How will you ensure that you have sufficient knowledge about the business situation? Too often, leaders assume they have all the information, so they may discount or even ignore information that does not fit with the overall strategy.

- Discuss the current levels of credibility, trust, and respect that you and your leaders have with the organization. What are your strengths? What's missing?

- Determine how you will lead in this situation. Which actions will you take to help people get engaged to "want" to make the changes? Figure 17 provides behaviors to lead successful change. Discuss the leadership behaviors that you and your team will use to coach, reinforce, and shape the new way.

- Map out the plans to prepare leaders to lead the change through communications and other actions. Figure 15 provides a checklist of items to create a Leader Communication Toolkit. Additionally, ensure that all leaders are engaging in the right actions to yield the desired results (Figure 20).

- Which of the Five Keys for Leading Change may you and your organization use in the preparations and execution of your change initiative?

7. Engage and Build Accountability

- Define and cultivate new behaviors, the new actions that will drive the results. Define the actions required to implement the solution. Go one step further and match the leadership behaviors to support these new actions. Use Figure 21 to develop behavior-shaping plans from the ground floor to the C-suite so everyone is working in concert to implement the changes.

- Understand and address the challenges and obstacles that will get in the way of performing new actions.

- Identify the natural resistance, concerns, and fears that come with asking people to step out of their comfort zone. Discuss where people may get "stuck" or resist the changes, and determine what you as leaders will do to deal with such resistance. Figure 22 provides a way to name the resistance and capture plans to focus and engage people in working through the physical, mental, and emotional aspects of change.

- What evidence will you be looking for to indicate that people have adopted the changes?

- How can you break work up into smaller tasks, so people can stay focused and productive during the transition?

- What can leaders do to reinforce and support the new way? Discuss your and your leadership teams' coaching and feedback approaches to shaping new behaviors.

- Where might you and your leadership team struggle in implementing the solution through others? What resistances or reactions may you leaders exhibit in this transition?

8. Develop a Roadmap and a Timeline

Prioritize, map out, and sequence leadership actions to ensure that the change stays the course.

- Create a leadership timeline with key touchpoints. Map out pre- to post-implementation actions, especially if leaders may not follow through on the plans. Use Figure 12 as an outline to map out the key leadership activities.

- Review the project plan to identify key touchpoints, key milestones, and areas where people may need to be engaged in the process. Take this information and create a leadership activity timeline over, say, 30, 60, 90, and 180 days—also known as the roadmap.

- As you work through the components of the Toolkit, capture key milestones and leadership actions in the roadmap.

- Incorporate other critical leadership deliverables into the roadmap to prioritize and sequence activities so that you streamline actions and eliminate duplication or conflicting messages.

- Review the roadmap to indicate interdependencies.

- Populate and expand the roadmap throughout the implementation.

- Incorporate communications—both the Big "C" and the important reinforcement little "c" communications.

9. Measure Progress and Results

Create a measurement dashboard to collect qualitative and quantitative evidence that the change effort is on track. Incorporate leading indicators into your dashboard so leaders know what needs their attention. Figure 23 provides questions to help you create your dashboard.

- What will you be measuring?

- What are the leading indicators that the changes are starting to take hold? What evidence of individual and group actions will you look for that will let you know you are on track?

- How will you use measurement to reinforce the new way?

- What will you do to celebrate small progress along the way so that people stay energized and engaged?

- How will you use measurement to ensure that the Five Keys for Leading Change are achieved?

10. Assess the Results

- How will you celebrate the small achievements on the way toward the larger goals?

- How will you stay engaged to ensure that the results "stick"?

- How will you handle setbacks, so that your and your team's messages are consistent and will accelerate positive outcomes?

- How will you capture the lessons learned and then incorporate this approach in other work?

Case Study: What Really Happened at MergeCo

The Scenario

Let's take a closer look at the case study in the book and discuss both what actually happened at MergeCo and what the leadership could have done to make the integration successful.

The merger was hailed as "a marriage of equals." The NorthCo CEO was quoted as saying, "By combining and utilizing each other's strengths, we have a preeminent position to expand into new markets that will benefit our customers and improve value to our shareholders." Another business journal quoted the SouthCo CEO as predicting, "If this merger is going to work, human factors will be of paramount importance."

At the end of the first year, neither prediction was true. As you've read in the case study, the integration of MergeCo never quite got off the ground. One year later, its share price was less than the sum of its parts. Customers felt frustrated. Employee morale was low. SouthCo executives were even defecting to competitors. MergeCo's CEO blamed the issues on weak sales and out-of-control costs occurring since the merger.

MergeCo was firmly in control, but it made only a few changes in its business approach. Legacy SouthCo employees struggled in this unfamiliar environment, and their NorthCo leaders were ill-equipped to lead the integration changes. MergeCo's CEO admitted that the original plan was to take over the former SouthCo business and treat it like a business unit. The deliberate deception was a smoke screen to get SouthCo leaders to accept the deal. That backfired. This deception shattered the expectations and confidence of management, employees, customers, and shareholders.

At the request of the Board, an executive task force was chartered to stop the hemorrhaging and deliver value. Their assessment was that it would take two to four years to turn things around. However, approximately three years after the merger, MergeCo was in weakened financial condition. It then announced that it would spin off the SouthCo business.

Because of NorthCo's solid northern industrial customer base (most of which remained with it through the merger period), it was able to regain profitability and financial health. After the split, it looked for a smaller company to *acquire*, one more culturally and philosophically similar to it than SouthCo and one that could open doors to global expansion.

SouthCo never regained financial health or its marketplace position. Too many key executives had left; most of its employees had been laid off or decided to leave. Customers who had been glad to work with SouthCo felt ignored or mistreated by MergeCo. With its branding confused and its organization disrupted, MergeCo's Board agreed to look for a *merger* partner in the spinoff, one that the former

SouthCo could grow with, while maintaining the culture and way of doing business it favored.

What Went Wrong?

While both companies made industrial equipment, the similarities ended there. The problems started at the very beginning, when the two CEOs looked at the potential financial gains of a merger, without considering the vast differences between the two companies. As we saw in the case study, the leaders elected to continue to lead the way they did in their respective companies. They ignored the key rule of leading strategic changes (including mergers): The cultural and human factors determine whether a change effort will succeed or fail. Without attending to the people aspects of the integration, MergeCo was never able to combine the businesses.

As we saw in the case study, the differences in management style were dramatic. NorthCo used top-down management and communicated on a "need to know" basis. By contrast, SouthCo employed a creative, freewheeling approach built on empowerment and consensus management that had enabled fast growth. Was it even plausible that it would be easy to integrate the companies as a "merger of equals"? In hindsight, probably not—especially considering the way that the leaders approached the task.

The eventual unraveling of MergeCo was a direct result of mismanaging the people aspects of the business, including: leadership philosophy, employee engagement, decision-making, setting a clear strategic direction, and communications.

Aside from the announcement, MergeCo shared minimal information with leaders and employees about what was happening. This created confusion, resistance, and a reduction in productivity throughout both organizations. It's unfortunate that the MergeCo leaders didn't have the benefits of knowing how to address the Five Keys for Leading Change and the companion tools that could have helped them successfully lead the change.

As was evident in the case study, many business and functional areas were left to figure things out for themselves. R&D was one of the few areas that found benefits in sharing best practices. Unfortunately, the combined supplier savings did not pan out, as it was difficult to sort out each company's different material specifications. MergeCo did integrate the sales force, but often had sales representatives from both companies calling on the same customer. As a result, customers became frustrated and were disappointed with the service. The expected benefits of greater marketplace presence and smoother distribution logistics simply never happened.

Despite the work by integration teams, the different business cultures created a distraction that was never addressed. Former NorthCo executives acted as if nothing had changed. Integration teams and functional leaders focused more on the business content, and not enough time or emphasis was spent on the people aspects of the integration. Leaders expected people to carry out new actions because they were told what to do. Little time was spent focusing on "how" to execute the changes in a way that helped people understand their role and "want" to make the merger work. Neither side showed enough willingness to change. The struggle to make decisions, personal agendas, and politics all stalled efforts.

In the end, millions were spent, careers were ruined, and the deal fell apart. Had MergeCo focused on people and cultural aspects, would it have been in a different position today?

The Solution

How Could MergeCo Have Been Saved?

One could argue that the initial decision to merge these two companies was flawed. Others might may say that, with the right cultural integration and leadership plans, MergeCo could have achieved its goals.

The case study outlines many of the challenges MergeCo faced. Here are five quick tips regarding how MergeCo could have used the Five Keys for Leading Change as well as the Toolkit to surface issues and create integration plans that addressed the cultural differences.

1. **Case for Change** – It became clear that the leadership was not in agreement about either the acquisition strategy or the integration strategy. Only much later did the MergeCo CEO admit that the deal was an "acquisition" made in the expectation that SouthCo would just be one of the MergeCo business units. Had the leadership developed a real case for change, the differences and challenges would have been surfaced at the beginning. The case for change could then have acted as a starting

point to brainstorm the people and cultural challenges that would close the gap to absorb SouthCo into NorthCo as a business unit.

2. **Assessing the Business, People, and Organizational Impacts –** If MergeCo had created a business, people, and organizational assessment, the similarities and differences would have surfaced. Often these assessments are created, but leaders do not spend enough time discussing the implications and the leadership actions to mitigate the risks. When leaders review the cultural and people impacts in a pre-acquisition assessment and a roadmap, they can see the disparities and come up with plans to close the gaps before completing a deal. The key is for leadership to take these findings and talk through "how" they plan to execute the change. When executives facilitate these conversations, they start to see where the challenges in execution will occur.

3. **Communications, Engagement, and Leadership –** Beyond the initial announcement, MergeCo leaders were simply not engaged. The lack of communication caused wasteful uncertainty. Imagine the cost and loss in productivity if each employee spent even one hour a day trying to figure out what was going on and what actions they would take. The Five Keys and the Toolkit provide a time-tested approach to incorporating the people side of change into the execution of strategic initiatives like MergeCo's integration plans.

These tools help leaders focus and lay out practical and actionable plans that engage the organization. These plans work because the leader has taken the time to create a people strategy and plan and is committed to executing that plan. In the case of MergeCo, the problems started with the pre-acquisition negotiations. The NorthCo CEO lacked transparency and honesty about the vision of the acquisition. When leaders are afraid to tell the truth, they create trust issues, which result in more churn, loss of productivity, and employee turnover. It's always better to be transparent and up front and to let people quickly make decisions on whether to stay or go. Leaders who pay attention to the communications, prepare leaders to cascade messages, and work to reinforce and engage people find their delicate, sensitive change challenges become non-events.

4. **Measurement** – Beyond the integration synergy targets, it's not clear that MergeCo established intermediate goals to keep people focused and moving ahead. Setting clear, attainable goals and measuring progress toward results enables people to know what is expected of them. Then they are in a much better position to be part of the solution, versus acting as an unintended roadblock.

5. **Leadership Roadmap** – If the MergeCo executives had outlined even a short 30-, 60-, or 90-day timeline postclose, they could likely have aligned the leadership actions throughout the organization to coordinate work as a combined entity. Instead, those leaders chose their own individualistic approaches, which most of the time weren't in the best interest of the combined entity. A roadmap helps leaders trace out their roles in the change and decide where they need to be engaged. The roadmap helps leaders determine where to be and how to make a

positive impact. In the case of the MergeCo CEO, he never visited the key SouthCo facilities and he left the messaging up to others.

If you are going to merge, reorganize, implement a new strategy, or create another change initiative, be willing to lead the strategic, tactical, and people aspects of the implementation. Often, leaders miss or avoid the people aspects, regarding them as intangible and difficult to address. Yet if you don't address the people aspects of change, you create confusion and chaos, which eventually leads to failure. A leader's role is to deliver results effectively and efficiently through people. Failure to engage with people results in business failures. If the two companies had taken the time up front, they may well have still been in existence as MergeCo.

Appendix C

Case Study: Making Acquisitions Work

This case study lays out the actions that leaders took to ensure the success of their merger strategy. The leaders paid special attention to mapping out leadership actions to keep their people focused and engaged during the transformation of the business. As you will see, their efforts paid off.

The Scenario

It took a year to get regulatory approval, but finally the successful merger of equals between two industrial companies—among the largest in the world—was complete. "Today marks a significant milestone in the histories of our two companies," said the Chairman (dialogue fictionalized). "We move forward to create a merger of equals that will drive growth for the benefit of all stakeholders." The two companies were close competitors and rivals in the marketplace, and were very familiar with each other's strategies, capabilities, and talents.

The Solution

Developing a clear case for change. Before the merger, the two companies built their case for change, which included the following points: The merger would create more opportunities for both companies going forward. It would increase the resources available for innovative product development. And it would strengthen the finances of the combined entities by sharing expensive fixed assets. In sum, the merger would strengthen both companies and create one organization with greatly increased resources and abilities to compete in the marketplace. The leaders used the case for change to convert the merger strategy into language and actions, so that all leaders, managers, and employees understood their roles and knew what to do.

Analyzing the business, people, and organizational impacts. Both sides recognized that their cultures were similar in many ways: Both reflected high safety standards, concern for the environment, and commitment to long-term shareholder value, which would aid in merging the businesses. But there were differences in business approaches and processes that required special attention. One company was more hierarchical and risk-averse, while the other was empowering and entrepreneurial; one company rewarded individual performance, while the other was team-oriented. Leaders from both sides agreed to focus on the similarities as the starting point for building the merged company. They then worked through the differences, to come to agreement about how to operate the company going forward. In some cases, they chose one company's approach; in certain instances, they chose the other; and in some situations, they created an entirely new practice or process.

Crafting a leadership roadmap. The year-long regulatory approval process between the announcement and close gave the leaders time to plan thoroughly. The leaders set up multilevel teams to handle merger activities, while focusing leaders throughout both organizations on keeping the businesses running. They created a Toolkit: It provided all leaders with tools to help them communicate well and work with their people, enabling everyone to understand what was happening, what their roles would be going forward, and how their daily work would change. The leaders were briefed on their level of authority to take action and make decisions, which made all the work run smoothly.

Building engagement to shape new behaviors. Because both sides were well aware of the cultural differences, the leaders worked on developing an approach to engage their people in working in the new way. Executives mapped out plans for bringing the two companies together. Local managers were trained to recognize resistance and were given ways to encourage their people to want to become part of the change and to participate in the change activities.

Communicating strategically. From the announcement to post-integration, the leaders spent a great deal of time communicating about what was happening across the organization. Beyond the formal announcements, they held informal discussions in brown bag lunches, group sessions, and team meetings. One regional executive developed what she called a "hearts-and-minds" program, which was quickly adopted throughout the company. Leaders were kept informed and asked to cascade information. Extensive resources were made available to help leaders answer questions.

The Outcome

Over the course of the first year, the top leaders monitored what was happening throughout the merging organization.

The merger teams and the functional executives established business and integration goals. Leaders reviewed progress monthly and kept the organization informed. Leaders were encouraged to communicate problems as soon as they arose and were able to draw on a pool of resources to keep all activities moving forward. From the executive C-suite to the shop floor, everyone played a critical role in keeping the business performing while integrating the operations.

At the end of the first year, they were ahead of plan. In addition to achieving the business targets, leaders throughout the organization were working collaboratively to chart the course for years to come. The initial merger was deemed a success.

When thinking through what had happened to make the merger work, the top leaders identified the following factors: clarity of mutually agreed upon goals; a well-defined organizational structure with defined responsibilities and authority; understanding what was important; and moving quickly to combine the organizations. Leaders played a significant role in paying close attention to what was happening and solving problems as they arose. Perhaps most important was the consistency of leadership by mapping out leadership actions and cascading messages. Leaders knew from the start what they were creating, why they were creating it, and how everyone would benefit from the change.

Appendix D

Case Study: Driving Successful Reorganizations

The following case study is about a consumer package goods business and its journey to reorganize and implement a strategy for refreshing market segment innovation and growth. At the end of the case study, discussion questions will help you reflect on how this company used the Five Keys to successfully lead the transformation of its business.

The Scenario

For decades, this 50-year-old consumer packaged goods company has been a staple in homes across the globe. Over the past several years, sales revenue from its traditional products have been declining and the company missed its projected growth targets. The company was losing new consumers, who were looking for healthier, environmentally friendly products. If the company hadn't run several cost-reduction programs last year, it would not have achieved its earnings targets.

Sales revenue was far from the only challenge. The company was still recouping from a regional product recall, which had tarnished its stellar reputation. This recall came at the same time when its strongest competitor introduced an enhanced, better-tasting, less expensive product with new, environmentally friendly packaging.

The Board was putting pressure on the CEO and the management team to turn things around. Several influential Board members expressed interest in acquiring a small, natural products company to inject new growth ideas and revenue into the company. The CEO didn't agree and eventually resigned due to philosophical differences. A new CEO was hired from the outside, a leader with a track record for bringing innovative, profitable growth.

"Fred," the new CEO, entered the role knowing that significant changes to the strategy and organization would be required to turn the company around. He used his first 120 days to learn about the business, build key relationships, and assess how to lead the strategic changes that were to come. Fred was concerned that several on the team might see the organizational changes as a reduction in their responsibilities and therefore their career opportunities. Furthermore, underlying cross-organizational tension created functional silos, which caused numerous problems. Functional goals and targets didn't always line up to deliver the business targets. The Head of Sales complained that the plant couldn't keep inventory on critical products, while Operations blamed the problem on the sales forecast. Simply put, the supply-and-demand forecasting system was broken.

The functional organization structure did not support cross-organizational collaboration. Any actions seemed to require some heroic effort, and, fortunately, many people rallied under the pressure, though this way of operating was taking its toll on the organization. Leaders spent most of their time fighting fires versus working on the next generation of products and solutions. Open positions had not been filled, and the organization lacked the pipeline of talent for critical roles; the last few hires had come from the outside. The Chief Marketing Officer oversaw all brands, with all decisions funneled up to the top. Instead of developing marketing growth strategies, most of the CMO's time was spent handling daily tactical matters.

The Solution

New Business Team Orientation

Fred chartered a small, strategy design team to map out both a growth strategy and an organizational structure for each of the major product categories, which would move accountability and decision-making down throughout the organization to its lowest level. The goal was to create collaborative, innovative, cross-functional business teams focused on products, so as to create growth organically as well as through acquisition.

The business team concept was aimed at putting more attention on the product groups within the portfolio. The intent of the new structure was to create the best of both worlds. It was designed to encourage cross-functional collaboration within an individual business area, while functional representatives would report into functional centers of excellence. Five new multidisciplinary business teams would be created to work on common business goals and align with product areas and consumer preferences. The company would maintain two stand-alone businesses, which were already working as intact business teams. The new structure would enable business growth while providing opportunities for new leaders to emerge.

Fred felt strongly that his organizational model would drive accountability and quicker decision-making into the various brands business teams. Because decision-making was pushed to the business teams, each product area could become faster and more agile at growing their product.

The business teams would be charged with the development and execution of the business strategy and would have full P&L accountability. Each business team would be led by a general manager, often a Marketing Vice-President. Team members continued to report directly to functional VPs to maintain functional excellence, with dotted-line responsibility given to the General Manager. The business team orientation was expected to:

- Organize and delegate responsibilities to match actions with customer and consumer needs
- Create a sense of ownership with clear accountability
- Provide opportunities for developing talent and building a robust talent pipeline

While business teams led the business areas, functional leaders would continue to build and execute functional plans, define standards, staff the teams, and ensure that members received appropriate coaching and development. Employees were to be rewarded on the company's overall performance. Business team members would have the opportunity to enhance their bonus compensation through delivering against their business team and individual objectives.

While the solution made sense, the team recognized that a recent six-year history of failed reorganizations and missed targets could taint the implementation, because employees might be skeptical. Since the company had a history of failed initiatives, Fred and others felt that personnel could easily misinterpret these changes as yet another "annual talent reduction exercise." Leadership support and employee engagement would be the keys to success.

Fred knew that the commitment and engagement of the senior management team would be pivotal to the success of this new strategy. That team would be accountable for the divisional strategy, governance, metrics, and resource allocation. Timing was critical to realize results by year-end.

Considerations

The CEO and the design team were anxious to get started. They knew that the enrollment and engagement of the senior management team was critical to cascading the new strategy and structure. The design team anticipated the very questions from these managers about how it would all work.

Because of the company's history of annual reorganizations, people felt wary of yet another new initiative that could soak up a lot of time and might not yield results. The number of employees declined, but the work never went away. The employees who remained were expected to fill the void. The new business team concept was intended to build the leadership pipeline and create opportunities; however, the CEO knew he needed to grab people's attention before they heard the word "reorganize" and didn't listen to the rest of the message.

The senior management team was concerned that, with so many projects under way, they would need to help people prioritize and focus on the key activities. There was also a pending global Enterprise Resource Planning (ERP) implementation, which would affect everyone's work. The team discussed the risks and the actions for mitigating the risks to keep people focused on the daily business, while implementing a new approach.

Not everyone would see the benefits of these changes. Some would misinterpret the hiring of a new Marketing VP from the outside as a loss of confidence in managers coming up in the ranks. Fred and his team were concerned that valuable players could leave the company because they perceived the change to a business team structure as taking away responsibilities and reducing their opportunities for advancement. The leadership team would need to demonstrate that they were passing decisions to the business teams and that this approach would work. The skeptics would be asking questions about the benefits of this approach and how this structure would contribute to growing the business. So, the team talked about how to communicate and to engage the management team first, then to ask them to be part of the announcement and implementation. They started to make a list of the key people, focusing on those roles most affected by the business team structure.

Communicating to the Top 100

Fred decided to use the company's upcoming Top 100 Leadership Meeting to communicate the strategy and structure. The meeting would be a working session, versus the typical two days filled with only presentations. The goal would be to communicate one-on-one with each participant before the meeting, so that the meeting time could be spent on working the issues. Senior management was intimately involved in the preparations. They started to craft a leadership roadmap to provide a visual picture of the leadership roles and actions, ranging from announcement to implementation.

While Fred wanted to jump in and discuss the strategy, his head of HR reminded him that people would first want to hear what was happening to them personally, before they would want to hear about the new growth strategy. So, the small team drafted a case for change to communicate the strategy and organizational changes in terms people could understand. They assessed the changes against the other business elements and recognized that adjustments were required in several areas, including: ways of working, ways of realigning business decision-making processes, and ways that people would be compensated and rewarded in the revised roles.

The transition from design concept to the new way would take thoughtful planning, communication, and implementation. Fred knew his leadership team needed to act differently to successfully move from concept to the new way. People would be listening for career opportunities, proof that this wasn't a cost-cutting exercise, and clear definitions of roles where they could succeed.

Senior management team members needed a moment to process the changes. The Chief Marketing Officer felt she was losing part of her current role. Operations and R&D were afraid that, with marketing leading the business teams, their functional voices would not be heard. Some leaders were concerned that they lacked the talent to place people on the business team in decision-making roles. The group worked to answer the many questions and shape the communications into an outline that could be cascaded to leaders throughout the organization.

Each leader developed individualized communications to review the changes one-on-one with their direct reports. Senior managers met with each attendee before the Top 100 meeting to share the plans and the impact on the direct report. This gave the leaders a head start, as people came to the meeting ready to work on implementation plans. The critical keys were to:

- Outline the new strategy and structure

- Define people's roles and responsibilities

- Gain agreement and acceptance of the new strategy and organizational design

- Define the new ways of working and the new decision-making protocols

- Address questions and concerns

- Outline communications by department, function, and region

- Engage people so they would want to drive profitable growth in this new model

Excitement within the Top Leadership team was starting to build. The senior management team agreed on the following implementation behaviors, which were cascaded to other managers:

- Understand the changes. When in doubt, seek clarification.

- Listen and observe to identify what's working and what's not.

- Solve problems, address concerns, and answer questions.

- Give plenty of positive feedback and create learning opportunities.

- Increase communications and give clear direction to keep people focused.

- Model the new roles and visibly support the changes.

- Celebrate small wins and advances.

Company Announcement

Following a town hall announcement, leaders shared the changes in small groups and one-on-one meetings, using a consistent communication package. Business team start-up sessions quickly followed. HR organized ways to keep the channels of communications open. Regular information meetings were promoted and held. Pulse-check surveys were conducted monthly, with quick-fix actions taken as needed. Feedback suggestion boxes were posted both onsite and online. A special Intranet site was added to provide updates and tell success stories.

Business Outcomes

As a result, the announcement and deployment of the business teams were deemed a success. People rapidly bought into the new model, wanted to discuss more about how to operate the business teams, and wished to understand how to participate in executing the new business strategy. Here are a few of the "quick wins":

- Post-announcement, 85% of employees understood the changes and appreciated the communications.

- 60% of the employees felt excited about the new direction.

- Business teams were up and running in the first 30 days.

- The innovation pipeline grew.

- The business exceeded its targets for the year.

- Year-end bonuses were paid—a first in many years.

Case Study Discussion

You have been named a member of the small team to craft the implementation plan. As part of this team, respond to the following questions, using the Toolkit components to prepare to lead the changes.

1. Use the Case for Change to translate the strategy and new organizational structure into language that accelerates the changes.

2. Discuss the impact that a new growth strategy and organization structure will have on other business elements. What areas would you recommend that the team review?

3. Which people should the CEO and team pay special attention to, and which organizational changes should they anticipate? How should the CEO address the transition from the current ways of working to the new business team approach?

4. What are some topics that the CEO will need to address to gain agreement and alignment with the senior management team? Where do you think the management team will struggle to get aligned?

5. Which questions or objections should the CEO be prepared to address both with the management team and in one-on-one conversations?

6. Set out a communications plan, starting with the engagement of the senior management team, that will build agreement, acceptance, and action.

7. Which issues would you recommend that the CEO and team pay attention to, so they don't lose the growth opportunity?

8. Which issues do you think the company will encounter in the implementation of the new structure? Use your list of issues to answer question 9.

9. Discuss how you would lay out a leadership change roadmap to help the leaders identify the critical touchpoints for successfully engaging in and then executing the changes.

10. What measurements would you use to determine whether the initiative is successful? Set out a plan for measuring, assessing, and adjusting (as needed) the plans for implementing the change initiative.

Acknowledgments

Thank you to my clients, who teach me every day through your experiences and willingness to sweat the details to make the motivation and engagement of people a priority to achieving lasting results.

I am grateful to my family. Your love and support gives me the mojo to carry on. To my mom, who continues to transform and reinvent herself, which inspires me to realize that anything is possible. To my husband, Michael, who is a simplifier, always finding the most efficient and easiest path to get things done. To my son Garrett, and his girlfriend, Kellie, their inquisitive questions help me put into perspective how leadership messages actually get interpreted throughout an organization. And to my youngest, Evan, who reminds me everyday of the importance of living to a life purpose.

Thank you to my publishing team. Deirdre Silberstein, who in this third book has masterfully helped me create a case study format. To Lynn Amos of Fyne Lyne Ventures for the creative cover and interior design, Graham Van Dixhorn for strategizing how to make the book title and cover copy pop, and Mark Woodworth for his eagle editing eye, suggestions, and building fun into the process.

I am grateful to Christy Tryhus for holding me accountable throughout the process. Thanks to Tom Buford for your digital strategies and ideas.

To my colleagues and friends who over dinners, tea, and many conversations helped shape my thinking for this book. You know who you are. Your words of wisdom kept me forging ahead, while helping me see that my voice in serving others matters.

About the Author

Hilary Potts, founder of The HAP Group, is a change strategist who works with executives and their teams as they map out strategies to successfully lead and execute business transformations. Her work is built on a strong foundation of practical business experience, extensive consulting and executive coaching expertise, and deep transformational practices.

With over three decades of experience in leading and advising organizations, Hilary knows firsthand the importance of creating and implementing strategies to develop leaders and grow healthy companies. She has worked with thousands of leaders, implementing powerful principles and practices for achieving smarter, smoother transitions that drive business results.

She served as CEO and President of a global leader in performance-based consulting. She spent the first 15 years of her career at a Fortune 500 chemical company, where she held a variety of sales and business management positions.

Drawing on her business and consulting expertise, Hilary is the author of *The Truth About Change: A Leader's Guide to Successfully Executing Change Initiatives* and *The Executive Transition Playbook: Strategies for Starting Strong, Staying Focused, and Succeeding in Your New Leadership Role*.

For more details on how you can book Hilary for speaking events, consulting and coaching engagements, or workshop programs, visit her website: **www.HilaryPotts.com**.

Resources to Help You Lead Change

Are you interested in accelerating and sustaining results from your strategic initiatives?

Do you want to overcome the challenges with leading change?

To achieve lasting results starts with knowing you need to change-up your approach to meet the situation.

Take advantage of this opportunity and start right now!

Apply this practical and uncomplicated approach to lead yourself and others through challenging business times.

The Five Keys for Leading Change can help you see the gaps between your strategy and success.

Use the Toolkit components to engage your team to get everyone moving in the new direction.

Still looking for more help? For more resources, including downloads, articles, and blogs, visit **www.HilaryPotts.com.**

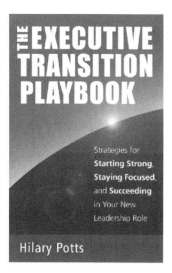

Don't just survive your leader transition. *Thrive* in it!

You are expected to get up to speed and add value to the business. *Fast.*

Hilary Potts offers powerful principles and practices to achieve a smarter, smoother transition. You will learn what to do and think about at each step, and will establish the platform for success well beyond your transition.

- Create a step-by-step plan to accelerate your learning and momentum.
- Know the classic transition mistakes and learn how to avoid them.
- Open communication channels and build trusting relationships across all levels.
- See even the subtlest warning signs that your transition is off track.
- Make clear, conscious choices about how you want to lead.

"Moving into a new role is a big challenge for any leader at any level. Read this book and let executive coach Hilary Potts help to make your leadership transition a smooth and successful one."

Ken Blanchard, coauthor of *The New One Minute Manager* and *Collaboration Begins with You*

Visit **www.executivetransitionplaybook.com** to download the first two chapters of *The Executive Transition Playbook*.

ISBN 978-1515360759 (paperback) US $19.95
Kindle, ASIN: B015QBK5BG US $9.99
Available on Amazon.com & Barnesandnoble.com

THE TRUTH ABOUT CHANGE

A Leader's Guide to Successfully Executing Change Initiatives

Hilary Potts

Close the Gap Between Strategy and Success

In business, change is the new normal. Yet leaders typically struggle to execute successful change efforts even when armed with a workable strategic vision. What's often missing is a practical leadership roadmap to help leaders know when and how to get engaged in leading the change effort.

The Truth About Change reveals the pitfalls that leaders encounter and lays out a clear path to success not found in change management or leadership books.

You'll discover how to:

- Organize and energize your greatest asset — human capital

- Gain agreement and support from day one

- Overcome the natural resistance to change to create a culture of engagement, accountability, and productivity

- Unite and inspire others to work in the "new way"

- Accelerate successful change initiatives now, and in the future

"Develop a competitive advantage by knowing how to successfully navigate and lead change."

Todd Lachman, President & CEO, Sovos Brands

"Simply brilliant—a refreshing, pragmatic blueprint for engineering effective change in your organization."

Brigadier General Thomas Kolditz, Director, Doerr Institute for New Leaders, Rice University

ISBN 978-1975745196 (paperback) US $19.95
Kindle, ASIN: B07663RBWW US $9.99
Available on Amazon.com & Barnesandnoble.com

Made in the USA
Middletown, DE
09 May 2019